ENDORSEMENTS

"In this 21-week Bible study, T. C. Stallings challenges us to take a hard look in the mirror and decide if we are a "participant" or "true team player" for Christ. What an awesome study to bring us closer to our Lord and Savior Jesus Christ."

RYAN RUSSELL

Director of Athletic Performance

Auburn University Football

"It's refreshing to see T. C. Stallings boldly living for Christ. His experiences as a former college and professional athlete give him the much-needed credibility within the world of athletics, which in essence, allows him to be his brothers' keeper. As iron sharpens iron, one person sharpens another (Proverbs 27:17). My prayer is that you will use this devotional to sharpen your spiritual skills, get you off the sideline, and fearlessly play on God's team!"

AUTRY L. DENSON, JR.

University of Notre Dame Running Backs Coach

"There are many examples of humility being a catalyst to greater success and happiness. Another is athlete T. C. Stallings."

RICK PITINO
Hall of Fame Coach

"T. C. is the big brother I wish I always had growing up. The type of man who always leads by example and does things in life the right way."

DEION BRANCH
Super Bowl MVP

"T. C. is a huge inspiration in my life. He showed me how to be a college Christian athlete when I needed it most."

BILAL POWELL
NFL Running Back

"T. C. speaks from experience and walks his talk. He enthusiastically connects with athletes, coaches, and sports fans of all ages!"

STEVE WIGGINTON
FCA National Director

PLAYING ON GOD'S TEAM

21-WEEK DEVOTIONAL FOR BUILDING
TRUE CHRISTIAN ATHLETES

T.C. STALLINGS

BroadStreet
PUBLISHING

BroadStreet Publishing Group, LLC
Racine, Wisconsin, USA
BroadStreetPublishing.com

PLAYING ON GOD'S TEAM:
21-WEEK DEVOTIONAL FOR BUILDING TRUE CHRISTIAN ATHLETES

ISBN-13: 978-1-4245-5364-8 (softcover)
ISBN-13: 978-1-4245-5365-5 (e-book)

Stock or custom editions of BroadStreet Publishing titles may be purchased in bulk for educational, business, ministry, fundraising, or sales promotional use. For information, please e-mail info@broadstreetpublishing.com.

Cover design by Chris Garborg, GarborgDesign.com
Interior design and typesetting by Katherine Lloyd, theDESKonline.com

Printed in the United States of America

17 18 19 20 5 4 3 2 1

Ailee —

Hope this book helps to inspire, encourage + build on your leadership for this year and off to Oregon. I'm so proud of who you are and what you are accomplishing in the sport + with your teams

You may one day hear your earthly coach say that you're one of the most dedicated players on the team. But when it comes to your dedication to God's team—which is the one that matters most— what kind of player would Jesus say you are?

—T. C. Stallings

can't wait to see you play at the next level! merry Christmas! 2017 Coach Jeff Fisher

CONTENTS

HOW TO USE THIS BIBLE STUDY AND DEVOTIONAL

This Bible study and devotional was specifically designed to help build, encourage, inspire, and produce committed and serious Christian athletes. It was designed for the purpose of producing true soldiers for Christ, not imposters, and real spiritual athletes, not fake ones. It was designed for men, women, boys, and girls who desire to consistently follow the game plan of Christ, not those who have become wishy-washy with Jesus, and who would like to stay that way. It is my desire that there are no more game-day-only Christian athletes. The call of God is about being an everyday follower of His Son, Jesus Christ, both on and off the field.

This Bible study is for athletes who not only want to be committed to their sports teams but are first and foremost interested in being committed to the team that matters most—God's team.

A Few Quick Training Tips Before We Begin

This study is challenging, and it covers a lot of Scripture. While this study can definitely be done alone, it is designed as a team study. Pushing through this experience and growing together as teammates, brothers and sisters in Christ, is highly encouraged and by far the best way to experience this twenty-one-week Bible study. But it's okay if you prefer—or you are in a situation that requires you—to tackle this study alone. The experience may be different but the outcome will be the same if you take it seriously. You will become a better player on God's team.

It is my desire that this would be a resource that empowers Christian athletes everywhere. I want you to confidently and courageously become the God-honoring, Christ-following athletes you were made to be, while letting nothing distract you, stop you, or stand in your way of following Jesus. For this reason, I suggest these tips as you power through over the next twenty-one weeks:

Always Pray First

Always begin with prayer. Every session. Every day. Pray for clarity and understanding. Pray about who you should involve in the study. Pray about who should lead this study (warning: it may be you!). And pray for the strength to finish this study and for the courage to attack the weekly training sessions with great determination. Also, pray for Jesus to speak to you in a life-changing way throughout and to help you dive deep into the challenging devotional sessions (called time-outs).

Group Format Suggestions

At this time, log on to www.tcstallings.com. On the "Playing on God's Team" page, watch the first video entitled "How to Use the POGT Team Bible Study and Devotional." If for any reason you cannot access the video, here is a quick summary of its contents. The Bible study consists of twenty-one sessions that are best experienced one week at a time to allow for proper retention and spiritual growth. Here is the suggested format for each session:

1. Opening prayer (one minute).
2. Discuss how everyone's week went in relation to the previous week's session (five to ten minutes).
3. The group leader may set the table for discussion by giving a short summary of the material for that day's session (this should take about two to five minutes).
4. Then discuss the passage, review the questions, and discuss as many answers to the questions as possible; be sure to review and discuss all the scriptures referenced (twenty-five to thirty minutes).
5. Watch the session wrap-up video (three to five minutes).
6. Final remarks and comments (two to three minutes).

7. Then take prayer requests and closing prayers (two to three minutes, or however the Spirit leads).

Each session is designed to take about an hour, but feel free to always let the Lord lead the group, making any necessary adjustments for tailoring the study to fit the needs of those who are attending.

A FEW MORE SUGGESTIONS

Make sure to watch all the wrap-up videos that the study provides. It's best to watch the videos just after the discussion time since they are designed to wrap everything up and bring closure to the session.

It is also important to involve as many of your teammates as you possibly can. The more accountability you have throughout the study, the better it will be. It's so awesome to grow together as a team.

And always remember to have fun! Getting better, stronger, smarter, and more committed to God's team should be extremely exciting for Christian athletes. Just as I enjoyed learning how to be a better football player, I also learned how to enjoy learning more about Jesus and being a better player on His team—even when I was challenged by some of the tougher lessons. Walking with Jesus isn't always hard, scary, or turbulent; following Him also brings laughter and joy. Enjoy these moments when they occur, for they will refresh and recharge your soul.

When I wrote *Playing on God's Team*, I had you in mind—the Christian athlete. Why? Because that's exactly what I was from age twelve to thirty-two, from a little league athlete all the way to the pros. Over this span of twenty years, I have learned what it truly means to play on God's team. Now, in a direct and challenging way, I am going to help make sure that you and your teammates understand this as well.

Are you ready to get started?

Okay. Enough warming up already—it's time to start training. Let's do it.

I'm proud to call you a teammate in Christ! In Jesus' name we pray, and on His team we play!"

—T. C. Stallings

Team Study Leaders

If you are a coach or player planning to be (or have been asked to be) the leader of a Playing on God's Team study group, I have a quick message to share with you before you start the first session. Please log on to www.tcstallings.com, and on the "Playing on God's Team" page, click on "Leadership Video" to view a short message for all group leaders.

YOU MUST HEAR THIS FIRST

During my college years at the University of Louisville, I had my reasons for thinking I was a good Christian. I was well known for my beliefs in college. I attended many Christian and faith-based events. I went to several campus-hosted Bible studies and even led one of my own. I even went to church on most weekends. I attended all the team chapel meetings (and even led many of them). And I was looked at by my peers as one of the only Christians on the team. In fact, whenever there was a request for a Christian athlete to represent my team, I was usually the player asked to do the honors. As a result of this, I was a proud Christian athlete—never the least bit concerned about my relationship with Jesus.

That is, until I discovered how bad it really was.

During my sophomore year, I was approached on

campus by a random student while heading to lunch. He politely asked if I would be willing to join him and his group for a campus Bible study. Hungry and in a rush, I quickly told him no thanks, and then I went on to explain that I already attended a weekly FCA Bible study and did not feel the need to attend another one. He politely stepped aside, and I went to lunch. But he wouldn't be dismissed that easily. From that day forward, any time he saw me, he kept suggesting that I attend his group.

Days later, we crossed paths once again. This time, however, he changed his approach. He boldly asked if he could come to my dorm room for a one-on-one study, promising that if I'd accept, he would not bother me about attending the group anymore. That sounded good to me! I just wanted the guy to move on and stop bothering me. How bad could one simple Bible study be anyway? So I quickly agreed to go to it.

Later that evening, he knocked on my door. He entered my room carrying his Bible and a videotape. Wasting no time at all (and probably sensing my impatience), he proceeded to pop in the tape. Fading in from black, the scene began. A soft worship song began, along with the sound of a whip snapping against flesh. I quickly sensed where this was heading. It was a well-done reenactment of the crucifixion of Jesus Christ. Soldiers were beating Jesus. Flesh was falling off His back. People were spitting on Him. He was brutally nailed to a cross and then lifted up. His face revealed His terrible agony. It was hard to watch. Sure, I knew the story of Christ … but this was tearing me apart. Why did we have to watch this?

Slowly, the screen finally faded back to black. Thank God, because I'd had enough. But then a few words began to slowly fade in and out: "Jesus paid the price for our sins … both yours and mine." Then more words appeared: "It was the sins of the world that put Him on the cross." One after the other, phrases kept appearing on the screen—and the point kept hitting home. I didn't know why he was specifically going this route … but what I did know is that I felt terrible.

When the video stopped, we got down to the nitty-gritty. He began to tell me what led him to me. It was really quite simple. I was a rising star on the football team with the reputation of being sold out for Christ. So he began to watch me on campus to see if I was in fact "the real deal." But I was not the real deal at all; I didn't even know what it took to be the real deal. What did *that* even mean?

When he used the words "real deal," he meant a true Christ follower. Not simply a "believer" in God, but also a true follower of His Son Jesus Christ. Being the "real deal" meant I was a person who had been changed by the Holy

Spirit, and then clearly lived a life that reflects the change. This sounded so new to me that I didn't even feel like a Christian anymore. I wasn't sure what I had been doing all of those years, but it certainly wasn't following Jesus, at least not faithfully.

How had I felt so comfortable for so many years? I was about to find out.

We opened our Bibles, and we began reading Scripture—probably more in an hour than I'd read all week. Verse after verse clearly confirmed that I was not a true Christ follower. This was hard for me to hear, that my relationship with Jesus—at least the one that I thought was solid—was lukewarm at best.

That's what drove this guy my way. He'd heard people refer to me as one of the best Christ-following athletes on campus, and he simply wanted to help me live up to that title. I will never forget the gist of what he said before he left that evening: "I know that you are known as one of the top Christians on the football team, and people look up to you as a result. You have a God-given platform … and I didn't want you to ruin it. That's why I felt led to share all of this with you, man."

Wow! I had nothing to say, and so I just sat there.

When he left my room, I got angry. I felt horrible about how much I had taken Christ's death on the cross for granted. I was embarrassed about how much Scripture I did not know. I thought I was a soldier for Christ, but then I realized I was not even a committed follower. That bothered me tremendously. It hurt me, too, because I misrepresented Jesus.

I didn't know that following Jesus was much deeper than a belief in God, carrying a Bible, going to church, praying over my food, and trying to avoid whatever is perceived as the "big" sins. I didn't know that the little things in life matter, like how I talked, what I thought in my head about girls, what music or movies I entertain myself with—that all of these things matter when it comes to following God.

I knew now, and I wanted to fix it immediately.

I begged God for forgiveness that night and promised Him that I would do my best to become a true follower of Christ. I'd read in Scripture, "You believe that there is one God. Good! Even the demons believe that—and shudder" (James 2:19). I was done just believing, because I realized that belief alone was not what makes us Christians. It only makes us believers! And so I decided that day that I wanted to be a Christ-following believer. I wanted to start living for Jesus, not just acknowledging that He exists.

However, I quickly realized that following Jesus was a whole different ball game than simply believing in Him. Anyone can believe, but only true followers passionately pursue the will of God. They strive to let His Son take over their entire lives. This was proving to be too tough of a task for me. Letting Jesus influence and dictate what I did in every area of my life almost seemed impossible. Failure after failure after failure—and I was trying really hard. I had thrown away my whole collection of foul-mouthed music, and I stopped having girls in my room at night. I stopped going to wild parties, and I avoided anything that seemed to dishonor God, no matter how tempting. But it wasn't long before my strong defense against temptation began to weaken. In no time at all, I was back sinfully engaged in the very things I was trying so hard to avoid.

On top of becoming weak, I was also beginning to lose friends. Since many of my teammates kept going to parties, drinking, lusting, and cussing, I had to pull back a bit, which left me alone many nights. Of course, parties in general were not wrong, and my friends were not evil demons who made me sin. But many of them were not pursuing God. And while God was renewing me, certain people and activities were just not the best for me at the time.

Resisting temptation was always hard, and it never seemed to get any easier! Each day I felt as though I was battling against the flesh, and the flesh was simply kicking my butt. It was frustrating because I truly wanted to change and become a solid Christ follower! But I could not beat temptation! Satan was dominating my mind, now more than ever before! I got upset with God about this because I was growing tired of always feeling so powerless. Where was He? Something was definitely wrong.

I had read so many verses about the "sin-stopping power" supposedly within us by way of the Holy Spirit. Well, mine must have been broken because I hardly ever felt any strength when facing temptation. So I lashed out at God in my dorm room one night, asking, "Where is the power? Why is this so hard? Why isn't the Holy Spirit showing up?" I ranted and complained, but nothing changed. I was close to giving up.

Don't get me wrong here: I wasn't close to giving up on Jesus, but I was close to giving up on being this super Christian who completely followed Jesus. I tried, and it was impossible. Maybe the dude who came to my room meant well, had the right idea, but he definitely set the bar too high and innocently misinterpreted the expectations of Jesus. I didn't really know what to think.

I knew one thing for sure: being a Christian was much easier before I had met him.

The Next Morning

I was watching *SportsCenter* in my dorm room on a Sunday morning, which was my regular ritual. On this day, however, the reporters were discussing different athletes and their amazing personal stories of triumph. The segment praised various athletes for their constant display of courage, dedication, perseverance, strength, determination, will, and passion. I loved watching these stories because I knew that I possessed the same qualities. This segment ended with one sportscaster saying something like, "These are the kind of players who all coaches want on their teams. They are winners. It's no wonder they are usually the players who become champions."

I was totally fired up after the show. I could clearly envision myself on that television screen being featured with all those athletes. I shared their same mind-set. My athletic DNA was 100 percent identical to theirs. I had the same kind of drive, that exact same kind of athletic will, and the same kind of passionate effort. I knew exactly why I was a successful college football player. It was because I gave my whole heart to the sport.

Focusing on football took my mind off my spiritual struggles momentarily, but I still wanted to get closer to Jesus. So I decided to get back into Scripture while I was in a good mood. I opened up my Bible and began to read 1 Corinthians 9:24–27 (NLT):

Don't you realize that in a race everyone runs, but only one person gets the prize? So run to win! All athletes are disciplined in their training. They do it to win a prize that will fade away, but we do it for an eternal prize. So I run with purpose in every step. I am not just shadowboxing. I discipline my body like an athlete, training it to do what it should. Otherwise, I fear that after preaching to others I myself might be disqualified.

After reading this, it suddenly hit me. A different thought came to my mind, a thought from the Lord. I imagined Jesus saying to me: "Sure, you are a great athlete, and yes, you do play well in the games. Do you know why? It is because you do everything your college football coach tells you to do. You play with incredible passion! You give a tremendous amount of effort to the Louisville Cardinal Football team … but what do I get? What kind of effort do you give me? What kind of player are you on my team? How passionate of a player are you for me?"

Boom. Just like that, I understood. My perspective changed instantly, and so did my life!

The Louisville Cardinals was not the only team I played for. By proclaiming the name of Christ as my Lord and Savior, I was also proclaiming my allegiance to God's team. To play well for the Cardinals, it always took sacrifice, dedication, relentlessness, courage, and passion. It was now clear to me that playing on God's team would require these same traits!

Team Jesus requires our best, it deserves our best, and it demands our best. Every player (or coach) on any team knows that poor effort will not produce victories. Well, playing on God's team is no different. Poor spiritual effort will only lead to spiritual losses. So it was clear why sin had my number. My effort toward Jesus stunk! A poor commitment to Jesus and the game plan of God will always end in defeat and frustration.

God was using Scripture to speak my language. The metaphors kept coming. If I wanted to play well in the game of life, then I needed to give my spiritual head coach everything I had. I needed to put all of my effort into doing what He asked of me as a player on His team. Jesus will never fail and will perfectly do His part as a coach. It was up to me to do my part as a player, which would always require my best effort. I knew I could not be perfect like Jesus, but I could be passionate. In either failure or success, my best efforts always needed to be put toward one extremely important thing: the Holy Spirit.

It is important to focus all your effort on getting to know what the Bible says about the power of the Holy Spirit, and then activate this power by letting Him take the lead in all areas of your life. This is where all your effort must be directed if you are to play for God's team, both faithfully and passionately. This is the key to all of your victories!

More on how our effort plays a role on God's team coming up soon. For now, however, we need to take a time-out.

⏱ TIME-OUT

Take a moment to reflect on what you just read. Below are a few discussion questions, but maybe some other questions have come to your mind as well while reading this. If so, then write them down and discuss them too. Pray and talk to God about all of them. Many of your questions may also be answered in upcoming chapters.

▦ DISCUSSION QUESTIONS

1. What stood out to you as you read Session 1?

2. Compare your commitment to your current team to your commitment to God's team. Which team do you feel currently gets your best efforts? Why?

3. Do you remember the student who watched my lifestyle for several weeks and then approached me about my faith? This resulted in me seeing that I had no clue of what it meant to truly follow Jesus. Imagine that someone has been watching you for the last

three weeks to see if you truly know how to follow Jesus. What would they think? What would they talk to you about?

4. On your sports team, you most likely make it a nonnegotiable top priority to do everything your coach tells you to do (as long as it is nothing dangerous, illegal, etc.). Is this the same attitude you have toward Jesus? Right now, is it your top priority to do whatever Jesus asks you to do? If not, then why? Do you think victories over Satan will come easier if you make following Jesus a nonnegotiable top priority?

▶ WATCH THE WRAP-UP VIDEO

To watch the wrap-up video, go to www.tcstallings.com, and on the "Playing on God's Team" page, click "Wrap-Up Vids." Then watch the video entitled Session #1: You Must Hear This First.

NOW, LET'S SET THE TABLE

Team is defined as a "group of people working together on a specific task." By definition, it is true to say that all Christians form a team. We are a group of people who are called by Jesus to work together with the common purpose of carrying out His will in the earth. With that understanding in mind, let's set the table for this Bible study by speaking a language all of us athletes can vibe with—let's talk in terms of a team.

Since we as Christians are indeed a team, then we can say that God is our head coach, along with His Son Jesus (who saved us) and His Holy Spirit (who empowers us). Since teams are designed to participate in games, we can say that Christians play in the game of life. This game schedule is a tough and lengthy one, however—365 days a year, seven days a week, twenty-four hours a day. We never stop playing because life never stops happening.

More than that, we play against the same opponent each day. Satan's team is powerful and determined. Their coach is crafty and clever. He is committed to his game plan of killing, stealing, and destroying (see John 10:10). He's playing to win, and he already has many victories. Just take a look at today's world and all the evil in it and you can clearly see how many lives he has impacted for the worse. Confidence when facing Satan can be hard to come by, which is why it is important that we always remember that "in all these things we are more than conquerors through him who loved us" (Romans 8:37).

This is so powerful to understand! We are more than conquerors. What does that even mean? I decided to look up the word *conqueror*. What I found was that there were multiple definitions, but here's the one I loved the most: "To be victorious."

That is simple. Romans 8:37 guarantees that even with all the power that Satan has in his arsenal, it is those of us on God's team who will ultimately be victorious. God's players will be the champions. There is nothing that can stop God's game plan from succeeding in the lives of His players—except one thing. What can stop His plan?

His own players. How is this even possible? We can

stop God's plan in our lives by abandoning His plan and doing our own thing. Jesus said, "I am the vine; you are the branches. If you remain in me and I in you, you will bear much fruit; apart from me you can do nothing" (John 15:5). Doing our own things means that we have abandoned God's plan.

Coaches Coach, Players Play

Many times, as players on God's team, the toughest battles we face in the game of life are the ones against ourselves. We get in God's way by not allowing Him to have His way. This is when we as players decide to take on the role of head coach. And in doing so, we replace God's plan with our own.

Take a look at John 15:5 and notice the word *remain*. It indicates and identifies a challenging task for each and every one of us—to not only let Jesus take the lead, but also to allow Jesus to keep that lead at all times. John 15:5 also reveals a key condition for all of us who decide to play on God's team: it is only through staying connected to God that the fruit-bearing occurs. He's making it clear that we'll never be able to accomplish anything meaningful for God without a connection to His Son.

Jesus knows that we may start off obeying His game plan but then be tempted to give up on it at some point. Jesus clearly warns that whenever we try to live according to our own set of rules, plans, or opinions, we are getting set to accomplish large amounts of nothing.

Are There Many Ways to Play on God's Team?

There is only one way to play on God's team—His way. Knowing that the game plan of Christ is the only one that will work for His team is an important aspect to grasp because we live in a world that tends to ignore this truth. Many people, rather than depending solely on the Bible's instructions, have chosen to trust their own instincts when determining what Jesus will or will not accept from them.

For example, this is how some athletes become what I like to call game-day Christians. They don't really pray or read Scripture that much during the week, but on game day, that's when God gets a lot of attention. I used to be like this myself. I wanted protection from injury, the vision on the field, and a victory all wrapped up in one big blessing. During the week, however, I just wanted my food blessed. I was not aware how silly it was for me to think that I could ignore Jesus all week long, and then—like a football genie—He'd grant all my game-day wishes just because I "believed in Him." It wasn't true of Jesus then, and it is still not true of Him today.

Many athletes in the world still try and pull this off. It's like they are trying to redefine the way following Christ works. However, no one can change what God's Word says and has already defined as acceptable when it comes to membership on God's team. Our earthly opinions will never be able to replace God-breathed Scripture. As a Christian, the Bible alone—without twisting, manipulating, or tailoring it—must be our ultimate source of truth and guidance. It alone is the completed perfect game plan of God. The Bible is the only acceptable way to play for His team. All other methods fail if they try to replace or compromise God's truth.

If life is the game, then the Bible is the perfect playbook. Much more on the playbook later, but for now, let me say this: without one, it is utterly impossible to play on God's team.

When people accept Christ and join His team but then make a lifelong continued effort to play by their own rules, they'll eventually become players He cannot use. By ignoring the game plan of God, you are cutting yourself off from the team. Jesus says it like this: "If you do not remain in me, you are like a branch that is thrown away and withers; such branches are picked up, thrown into the fire and burned" (John 15:6).

Choosing to live by our own rules is like walking up to Jesus and saying, "I'm sorry, Coach. I love being on your team, but I just don't like certain parts of your game plan. So

I'll just go with mine instead—but I'm still gonna need your blessings on my plans, Big Guy." If this is your approach to the biblical plan of God, then you need to consider yourself a withered branch disconnected from the tree. Nowhere in Scripture do we read about a Jesus who allows us to ignore Him yet use and abuse His power.

A Christian athlete is defined by the fact that he or she strives to follow Christ each and every day, because for each of them every day is game day.

You Get Out What You Put In

On any team, it is not the game plan alone that determines success, but also the effort given toward executing it. As Christians, we face an opponent who gives maximum effort every day. Satan's team plays with relentless effort bent on destroying the lives of Christians. Knowing this, what sense does it make for us to give poor effort in fighting back? Would you give poor effort toward preparing for a championship game in your sport—against the strongest team on the schedule—and still expect to win? Of course not. Poor effort doesn't produce wins for you on your sports teams, and it will not produce spiritual victories on Gods' team either—and we must never expect it to.

Well, the table is definitely set. It's time to dig in. Let's take a time-out, recharge, and get ready for the next session.

⏱ TIME-OUT

From here on out, I want you to think of Christians as individuals who form Team Jesus. This is God's team, and individual Christians are the players. Never forget that we are always playing as long as we are alive! And never forget that God, Jesus, and the Holy Spirit are always coaching.

It is important that we never take the game of life lightly! Satan, like any other opponent, would love for you to underestimate him. You have to be willing to give your best to Jesus and commit to His plan at all times. Sounds like hard work, right? Well, at times it can be. But as an athlete, we are no strangers to hard work. We know that it takes our best to be successful, to be a champion. Sure, it's hard work … but winning always makes it worth it. So plan to win at the game of life. Our coach has guaranteed us victory if we trust Him.

▦ DISCUSSION QUESTIONS

1. What are your thoughts about the fact that Satan is constantly at work, with the agenda of discouraging you? How might knowing this change the way you choose to prepare for the game of life each day?

2. Romans 8:37 says that we are "more than conquerors" in Christ Jesus. How does this make you feel when you read it? Do you feel like a champion spiritually? Why or why not?

3. If God, Jesus, and the Holy Spirit are your spiritual head coaches, how would you describe your relationship with all three? Is communication with them good or not so good? Why?

4. Do you feel like your life is currently mostly run by God's plan or your own? What changes need to be made to give Jesus complete control of your life?

▶ WATCH THE WRAP-UP VIDEO

To watch the wrap-up video, go to www.tcstallings.com, and on the "Playing on God's Team" page, click "Wrap-Up Vids." Then watch the video entitled Session #2: Now, Let's Set the Table.

WHAT WE DO MATTERS

Let your light shine before others,
that they may see your good deeds and glorify
your Father in heaven. —Matthew 5:16

This whole session can be summed up by Matthew 5:16. Read it again. What's one of the ways that God is glorified here on the earth? He is glorified by what we do. Jesus is the light and He lives within us. When we allow this light to shine for all to see, then good deeds happen and God is glorified as a result. For this reason, obedience to the Word of God matters, following Jesus wholeheartedly matters, and listening to the Holy Spirit matters. In fact, what we do in the game of life matters.

There are so many who claim to play for Christ but somehow got the impression that an "all-in for Jesus" attitude was not important, worth it, or even necessary. For them, occasionally acknowledging God ("I would like to thank God …") whenever something good happens is enough. But passionately pursuing obedience to the Bible with all they've got and doing everything Jesus commands is not a top priority in their lives. God does not approve of playing on His team in this way. In fact, here is exactly what He says about such people: "These people honor me with their lips, but their hearts are far from me" (Matthew 15:8).

Doing whatever we want with our lives without following Jesus is wrong—even if the choice results in something positive. Success alone is not the determining factor when it comes to pleasing God; the determining factor is whether or not Jesus led us to the success. The outcome of choices that are made apart from Jesus may at times please us, but they will not please Him.

God's Way or the Hell Way

Have you ever heard a coach who says, "It's my way or the highway"? It's just a cliché that simply means that the coach expects his plans to be executed by his players, and he will not tolerate players who try to take over or do their own thing. As players on a sports team, we've always understood this when a coach said it and so we simply fall in line. Of course there are always a few who test the coach's patience, and in many cases those players find themselves on the highway.

God's team is no different. It's His way or the hell way. In other words, it's what Jesus talked about in Matthew 7:21–23 (NLT):

"Not everyone who calls out to me, 'Lord, Lord!' will enter the Kingdom of Heaven, but only those who actually do the will of my Father in heaven will enter. On judgement day, many will say to me 'Lord! Lord! We prophesied in your name and cast out demons in your name and performed many miracles in your name.' But I will reply, 'I never knew you. Get away from me, you who break God's laws.' "

We cannot claim a spot on God's team, or claim Him as our coach, if we are not willing to play by His rules. Many who claim to be on His team are unfortunately fooling themselves, and they are in fact playing by their own sets of rules. They are calling their own plays and using their own personal opinionated game plans. It is an unacceptable hybrid form of faith that uses a half-world and half-Scripture blend of comfortable Christianity. This type of living does not allow God to take total control, Jesus to lead, or the Holy Spirit to form us.

Instead, it picks and chooses what parts of the Bible are relevant and which parts can be ignored. It allows people to openly and knowingly live contrary to God's game plan but still be allowed to claim membership on His team. This type of lifestyle may be one of the main reasons unbelievers reject Christianity. As a true player on God's team, we must avoid attempting to play in this way. If we do, we'll only end up playing on the wrong team. Jesus put it this way: "He who is not with Me is against Me; and he who does not gather with Me scatters" (Matthew 12:30 NASB).

If It Were Easy, Everyone Would Do It

Christians must back up our talk with our walk, which means our lives must align with Scripture. This is why many people try to create their own ways of being a Christian. It is much easier to obey our own rules, which are tailored to fit the type of lives we want to live, and to depend on our own self-sufficiency than it is to obey God's rules. Obeying God requires a complete lifestyle overhaul, allegiance to Christ, and a continual dependence on the Holy Spirit. No one said it was going to be easy, but it can be done. Jesus said that such a lifestyle is impossible for humans, but "with God all things are possible" (Matthew 19:26).

The Holy Spirit—if you put forth the effort of getting to know Him and staying close—will empower you to live as He commands. But let me warn you by reminding you that your own personal effort toward God's team—much like on your sports team—plays a huge role. If you say you are a Christian athlete, then you must live a life that backs up that claim. This is what will make a difference on your team, in your community, or in the world.

How much effort are you willing to give God's team each day? Your answer matters, because poor effort will not cut it. This should not come as a shock—you already know poor effort only produces failure. When is poor effort ever acceptable? Praised? Appreciated? Beneficial? Useful? Requested? Preferred? Recruited? Celebrated? Honored? Attractive? The answer is never—at least not by any organization that is planning to win.

No truly competitive championship-minded coach will ever make a habit of accepting poor effort from his or her players. In much the same way, our spiritual head coach is no different. He wants all we have to give, along with our best effort in giving it! Look at what God's game plan says concerning effort: "Love the Lord your God with all your heart and with all your soul and with all your strength and with all your mind" (Luke 10:27).

Do you see that? *All.* After all, there is nothing left to give! This is a straightforward commandment from God, demanding maximum effort while playing on God's team. We must love God with our entire beings. Whenever you—as a true Christian athlete—decide to serve God with all of your heart, soul, mind, and strength, and someone says to you, "It doesn't take all that," then I'd quickly open my Bible to Luke 10:27 and say, "Tell that to Jesus."

Show Me Some Love

It's a commandment in Scripture to love God with all the effort we have, but then we read this little motivator from Jesus: "If you love me, keep my commands" (John 14:15). Did we read that correctly? What we do when it comes to the game plan of God reveals how much we love Jesus.

It truly matters what we do in life. Have you ever met a player who loves his or her coach? They will run through a brick wall for that coach, right? In the same way, that kind of obedience to Jesus showcases our love for Him. Obedience to Jesus isn't always easy; however, if you want to show your love for Him, then obedience is a must. He knows it's hard to do with our own power, so He blessed us with His Spirit when we joined His team, enabling us to obey Him in an uncompromising way. This will always be the best way to show Jesus how much we love Him and to properly represent the team we play for.

Finally, let's look at what James had to say about the role of obedience and what we do in life. James wrote, "Show me your faith without deeds, and I will show you my faith by my deeds" (James 2:18). What you do says a ton about what you believe.

In this world, as players on God's team we must properly put the *do* back into being a Christian, because there is so much work to be done! It is a huge part of the plan of God, and even He feels that His team is falling short when it comes to putting in work. Jesus told His disciples, "The harvest is plentiful, but the workers are few" (Luke 10:2).

What we do matters. Don't let anyone tell you any differently.

⏱ TIME-OUT

Do you see why those of us claiming to be on God's team cannot afford to take our behavior lightly? It's not about being perfect, but about being passionate about properly representing our faith—our Lord, His Spirit, and our God! We've talked a lot about what we must do and how much it matters. But stay with me, because we are now going to talk about God's grace! However, this will not change what God says about your effort. Even with God's empowering grace, you will see that God is still crystal clear about putting effort into what He expects us to do!

▦ DISCUSSION QUESTIONS

1. How much emphasis do you put on obeying Scripture? Do you think it's possible to ignore the Bible yet still be blessed, highly favored, and guided by Jesus?

2. When we fail at sports and competitions, we usually get angry and plan to get better at whatever caused the failure. Describe what that same approach would look like when applied to sin and obedience?

3. No one can love God perfectly. But what steps do you need to take to feel as though you are doing all you can to love God with all of your heart, mind, soul, and strength? Does your sport or anything else in your life get all the effort you have to give? If so, why does this particular activity get your best?

4. How can you refrain from becoming a Christian who picks and chooses what parts of the Bible are relevant for your life right now, and instead allow the whole Bible to completely govern your life? What are your feelings about our need as players on God's team to live with complete, uncompromising obedience to Scripture?

🎞 WATCH THE WRAP-UP VIDEO

To watch the wrap-up video, go to www.tcstallings.com, and on the "Playing on God's Team" page, click "Wrap-Up Vids." Then watch the video entitled Session #3: What We Do Matters.

GRACE AND EFFORT

Grace is not opposed to great effort.
Grace should be the inspiration behind
your great effort. —T. C. Stallings

I find it interesting how much we ignore "the work part" of being a Christian, since that is one of the main reasons we were blessed with the Bible and gifted with the Holy Spirit. Both were given to us so we can spiritually know what God wants us to do and to have the power to do it (see 2 Timothy 3:16; Galatians 5:22–25). God makes it a point throughout the Bible to encourage us in obedience while promising to empower us to pull it all off. So why have we become so lazy and lukewarm with obedience in doing what God calls us to do? I believe it is primarily due to a misunderstanding of grace.

There are not enough words to describe the importance

of God's grace in our lives, but let's face it: we often abuse this awesome gift. Many use God's gift of grace as a way to justify not giving Him their best (shame on me if I am the only one who has ever done this!). We quickly reference Scripture (such as Isaiah 64:6) that likens our good deeds to "filthy rags." And we may even think this suggests that our best is useless—and you'd be right—depending on the context.

In terms of earning the love of Jesus, or in terms of creating salvation for ourselves, our deeds are absolutely useless. But when it comes to obedience to God, His Son, His Word, and His Spirit, our good deeds are far from pointless. Romans 6 (read it!) does a great job of describing how players on God's team should respond to God's amazing grace!

Misusing God's Grace

"Only God can judge" and "nobody is perfect" are popular statements often used to abuse and misuse God's grace. The statements are true in and of themselves, but we allow these truths to make us lazy when it comes to obeying the Bible. It's an easy mistake to make and a common habit that many fall into. Of course, these statements have a place in our faith because we are not perfect, God's grace is unbelievably amazing, and we are ecstatic that Jesus graciously paid the death penalty for our sins. However, if we genuinely appreciate God's amazing grace, and we are truly grateful and thankful for it, then that same grace should serve as the motivating factor behind all of our efforts toward pleasing God. We should be working as hard as we possibly can at obedience simply due to gratitude toward grace.

Works Do Not Earn Us Salvation

Salvation does not come by works. But just because deeds alone do not create salvation doesn't mean that they do not have a meaningful role to play when it comes to completely following Jesus. Problems arise whenever we try to use the comfort of our faith to hold back any effort toward biblical obedience. We must stop pitting grace, faith, and deeds against each other. Let the following scriptures sink into your spirit:

> You foolish person, do you want evidence that faith without deeds is useless? Was not our father Abraham considered righteous for what he did when he offered his son Isaac on the altar? You see that his faith and his actions were working together, and his faith was made complete by what he did. … You see that a person is considered righteous by what they do and not by faith alone. … As the body without the spirit is dead, so faith without deeds is dead. (James 2:20–22, 24, 26)

They Work Together

Earning salvation and showing appreciation for it through obedience are two totally different things entirely. Sure, our works cannot create salvation—grace already did that through the death and resurrection of Jesus Christ from the dead. But what we do with our lives represents the way we say thank you to Jesus for the work of His grace.

God gave us an undeserved, unearned invitation to join His team. There's our grace. After accepting the invite and joining His team, it's time to get in the game and play. That's our job. Effort and grace are two parts of our faith that must work together—they go hand in hand. Grace was, is, and will always be the work of Christ alone, while maximum effort toward obedience to the Bible is the work of Christians, who are empowered to do so by the Holy Spirit.

Grace is not opposed to great effort. In fact, it is the inspiration behind it!

⏱ TIME-OUT

God's grace is often misunderstood. Somehow, it gets turned into a license to sin or to live loosely. Hopefully, you properly understand that God's grace should not be abused but rather used as the fuel to strive for righteousness. Properly understood, grace is a beautiful thing. It is getting what we do not deserve, while living holy lives by the power of the Holy Spirit is giving Jesus what He deserves.

🔲 DISCUSSION QUESTIONS

1. How does your life say thank you to Jesus for His grace? In what ways does Jesus show grace to you daily? How are you responding with gratitude?

2. What do you think your life reveals to others about Jesus? About Christianity? About the Holy Spirit? Are what they learn from you helpful or hurtful to Christianity?

3. What has life been like for you since becoming a Christian?

4. Even with God's grace firmly in place, what does this verse personally mean to you: "Not everyone who says to me, 'Lord, Lord,' will enter the kingdom of heaven, but only the one who does the will of my Father who is in heaven" (Matthew 7:21)?

▶️ WATCH THE WRAP-UP VIDEO

To watch the wrap-up video, go to www.tcstallings.com, and under the "Playing on God's Team" tab, click "Wrap-Up Vids." Then watch the video entitled Session #4: Grace and Effort.

HEADS UP

Never forget the fundamentals. Before we power through the remaining sessions, we need to get back to the basics of our faith and remind ourselves of the commitment we made to God. This is what Sessions 5–7 will lead us into. We are about to take a look at how we first became members of God's team.

Looking back at this pivotal time in our lives will help refresh our minds concerning the spiritual expectation of playing on God's team. After we revisit this amazing process and relive God's grace in choosing us for salvation, giving Him our best effort in the game of life will become more of a priority. Sessions 5–7 combine to make one point, so we will not see another wrap-up video until the end of Session 7. See you there.

THE RECRUITMENT PROCESS, PART 1

By the time I was senior at Bedford High School in Ohio, I had become quite the running back. The college recruitment process was in full swing as hundreds of NCAA schools were in search of potential players.

Over five hundred miles south, in Kentucky, a group of coaches from the University of Louisville had their eyes on me. They were sitting in a room watching my highlight reels and reading my bio. They were sizing me up and breaking me down while critiquing my best and worst moments on the field. They started to imagine how I might fit in as a player on their football team. The more they watched me on film, the more they wanted me to be a Louisville Cardinal. I had never heard of the Louisville Cardinals and was unaware that they were making plans for me to possibly join their team. I had no idea they were recruiting me or that they even knew anything about me.

In a similar way, players on God's team are also recruited. Even while they know nothing about Jesus or His ways, God is planning on making them a part of His team. Psalm 139:16 (NLT) explains it this way:

You saw me before I was born.
Every day of my life was recorded in your book.
Every moment was laid out
before a single day had passed.

God chose you, and then He game planned your life! He knew exactly why He made you and what He wanted your purpose to be. He had already planned out how to use you on His team! He had big plans for you to play for His Son, and you didn't even know Him yet. Before you were even born or knew anything about God, He had already begun to spiritually recruit you. And after we are born and begin to live our lives, He continues the recruiting process. This is when we get to first hear about what God has for us through Christ!

Initial Contact

As the Louisville Cardinals continued to recruit me, the time soon came for them to notify me of their interest. The first attempt to connect with a player is called *initial contact*, which is usually done through a phone call or a letter in the mail.

When the coaches first made initial contact with me, I was excited, although I knew nothing about the University of Louisville and wasn't quite sure how to process the letters and the phone calls. As I regularly talked with them on the phone and listened to their plans, I began to grow more comfortable with the Louisville program. I loved hearing them tell me that I had great potential and could be a fantastic asset to their team. The head coach made sure I knew how much he really wanted me.

Jesus does much the same thing with His recruits. He speaks to our hearts and lets us know that He wants us on His team. Do you remember when you first experienced God's calling on your life to accept His Son Jesus and join His team? Do you remember hearing God's amazing plan of salvation? Well, He had been recruiting you since the beginning of time. He prepared a place for you on His team before you were even born, contacted your heart about it, and then He encouraged you to take hold of it.

I'm Not Good Enough

Unlike my college recruitment process, an impressive highlight reel of good moves is not required to gain the interest of Jesus. We need to rejoice that we did not have to play our way on to God's team, because that would require perfection! Thankfully, God never looks for perfect players. He only looks for willing ones—those who are willing to play hard on His team.

In fact, before accepting Christ, we were spiritually out of shape, spiritually slow and weak—yet Jesus did not pass us by! He remade us instead. Jesus can transform and train anyone, regardless of the type of life they lived prior to initial contact with Him. He knows that once He becomes the spiritual head coach of any player in any condition, He can remake him or her into spiritual superstars on God's team that exceed even their own expectations. The apostle Paul put it this way: "No eye has seen, no ear has heard, and no mind has imagined what God has prepared for those who love him" (1 Corinthians 2:9 NLT).

⏱ TIME-OUT

Hopefully you are starting to be reminded of what the beginning of your relationship with God was like. As we use this session and the next one to go through a reflective period concerning our salvation, do not let it bore you. The purpose of these throwback sessions will be revealed soon, and hopefully it will hit you like a ton of bricks. We never want to forget the moment our lives changed forever, when Jesus revealed Himself to us. He chose us, and we did nothing special to earn His choosing. This was all about Him, His grace, and His love.

⌖ DISCUSSION QUESTIONS

1. How did you first hear about Jesus? What was your initial response to what He had done for you?

2. What do you remember most about the moment when you first learned that you needed Jesus to save you?

3. On sports teams, it's usually the biggest, fastest, and most talented players who gain the attention of the coaches. What does it feel like to be chosen to be on God's team when in fact you were completely unqualified to play for Him?

THE RECRUITMENT PROCESS, PART 2

The Official Visit

College coaches make an official visit to a recruit's home once they feel that the player is ready to commit. A few months after initial contact from the Louisville Cardinals, the team soon scheduled an official visit to my home. I still remember being nervous when I heard them knocking at the door. My mother invited them in and we sat down to a meal she had prepared.

The coaches talked in great length and detail about all the plans they had for me. They elaborated on what position they wanted me to play and answered all of my questions. As I was getting to know them, this was also their chance to get to know me and get a feel for the type of person I was. The more we learned about each other, the better we were all beginning to feel. The most calming thing about this visit was hearing the coaches continuously remind me of how much they desired to have me on the team.

Jesus makes a spiritual "in-home" official visit to His recruits as well. At the time of His choosing, Jesus moves from desiring for us to join His team, to actively chasing us down to talk about it. Look at what it says in the book of Revelation: "Behold, I stand at the door and knock; if anyone hears My voice and opens the door, I will come in to him and will dine with him, and he with Me" (Revelation 3:20 NASB).

Jesus sends His Holy Spirit to knock at the door of our hearts and minds. If we open the door, then He will begin the process of revealing His game plan for our lives. I remember letting Jesus into my life. I recall opening the door to my heart and seriously listening to His plan—an amazing story that I can't wait to share with you later. (Do you remember when you first decided to let Jesus into your heart?) For me, it was the most freeing thing I had ever done.

When we let Jesus into our hearts, we can then begin to listen to Him tell us more about Himself, His Father, and His perfect plans for our lives. Paul wrote in Ephesians 2:10 (NLT), "For we are God's masterpiece. He has created us anew in Christ Jesus, so we can do the good things he has planned for us long ago." And it is at this official visit that Jesus shared these good things with you and with me!

The Offer

As my official visit with the coaches from U of L continued, it wasn't long before we started getting down to business. We talked, we laughed, and we got to know each other much better, but the main reason they were in my living room was to make me an offer. With my all-expenses-paid scholarship in their hands, the coaches extended to me the opportunity to join their team. Once the offer was made, they sat in total silence and patiently waited for me to answer.

As players on God's team, most of us can recall a similar experience. Once we let God into our hearts and He began His official visit with us, didn't He also make us an amazing offer to join His team? That offer was and is eternal life with Jesus, which is found in John 3:16 (NLT): "For God so loved the world that he gave his only Son, that whoever believes in him shall not perish but have eternal life." What a truly mind-blowing offer! We get an undeserved spot on God's team featuring a spiritually all-expenses-paid gift of eternal life! What a blessing indeed!

A scholarship was the only way for me to attend college, because I could not pay my way. The college paid all of my expenses because I played for their team. In the same way, you and I could have never spiritually afforded to pay for our own sins. But that didn't matter, because God paid off all of our spiritual expenses through the death and resurrection of His Son Jesus Christ. This was an unearned invitation to join God's team. John 3:16 represents God's great offer to join His Son's team. God held your heaven-ship in hand, made the offer of eternal life, and then waited patiently for us to answer with a resounding yes.

The Acceptance

The coaches had just a few more things to say prior to letting me sign on the dotted line. They warned me, before committing, to not only consider the good things ahead (a full scholarship, all expenses paid, televised games, etc.) but to also take into account the challenges that were sure to come. They clearly laid out both sides of the coin. They wanted me to unmistakably understand what would be expected of me if I chose to sign my name on the scholarship papers.

Essentially, I was asked to "count the cost" before joining the team. And so I began to consider everything that was discussed. After a few moments of reflection, I looked the head coach in his eyes and proudly asked for a pen to sign my scholarship. I accepted the offer and committed to the coach. At that defining moment, I had officially become a player on the University of Louisville football team.

Now let's look back at God's offer found in John 3:16. For Christians, this is the offer that we had to consider and eventually accept if we were to become a part of God's team. We spiritually signed on the dotted line by obeying this verse: "If you declare with your mouth, 'Jesus is Lord,' and believe in your heart that God raised him from the dead, you will be saved" (Romans 10:9).

Sounds Good to Me, Coach

Romans 10:9 is how you signed on the spiritual dotted line. You gave your life to Jesus Christ—and signed your heaven-ship. You accepted God's offer found in John 3:16. However, just as the college coaches laid out both sides of the coin, Jesus does the same thing in Scripture. He tells us about the forgiveness of sins, eternal life with Christ, and the awesome gift of the Holy Spirit (the good stuff!), but He also warns us of the challenges that are sure to come. Jesus promised that we would be persecuted for following Him, that we'd have to make sacrifices that might bring pain and suffering, and that while playing in the game of life, we would definitely have some trouble. He then challenged us to have joy when we face trials of many kinds. He even warned us not to become lazy or complacent so we could avoid unfavorable consequences.

Some of us may have missed this part of the deal when

we committed to Jesus because we only focused on the pleasant parts of being on His team. But it is a huge mistake to ignore what God says concerning counting the cost, because this important consideration prepares us for the sacrifices we will need to make while playing on His team. You don't pay to play on Jesus' team, but it does cost us. It costs us control of every aspect of our lives. Have you ever heard a coach say that he or she owns you when you joined the coach's team? Well, Jesus says much the same thing:

> Don't you realize that your body is the temple of the Holy Spirit, who lives in you and was given to you by God? You do not belong to yourself, for God bought you with a high price. So you must honor God with your body. (1 Corinthians 6:19–20 NLT)

As you read on, you will be able to determine whether or not you have fully counted the cost of membership on God's team. But for now it is important to remember that great moment of your acceptance of Christ's offer!

By accepting John 3:16 as the truth, and responding to it through Romans 10:9, Jesus granted us membership on His team. We then officially became players on God's team! Praise God, because this is such a wonderful gift. But this is where things get interesting.

⏱ TIME-OUT

We definitely will need to take a time-out at this point because things are about to shift into high gear. You will see what I mean as we transition into Session 7 and beyond. Meanwhile, take this week to really think about these last six sessions. Be reminded of the commitment you made to Jesus. Be reminded of what you signed up for. This is important, because the next sessions deal specifically with an area that many players struggle with—honoring the commitment.

▨ DISCUSSION QUESTIONS

1. What do you think it takes to be a successful player on your sports team? What about Team Jesus—what do you think it takes to be a successful player for Him?

2. What type of commitment does you head coach demand from you, and how do you respond? What, as far as you know from Scripture, are the spiritual demands that your spiritual head coach gives you? How do you respond to these demands from Jesus?

3. What happens if you ignore the expectations, requirements, demands, and the commitment requested from your head coach? What do you think happens when you ignore these same things requested by your spiritual head coach, Jesus?

THE RECRUITMENT PROCESS, PART 3

The Starting Blocks

Too many people think that accepting a position on God's team is the finish line, the end game. But I want to assure you that it is not. While it is definitely an amazing, uplifting, and beautiful life-changing decision, it is also only the beginning when it comes to playing on God's team.

The truth is that all spiritual athletes on God's team must understand this point: Joining Team Jesus meant just that— we actually *joined* His team. As amazing and as wonderful as this first step was, it is certainly not even close to the last step. It is nowhere near the finish line. It's only the starting line! This is why Paul wrote, "I press on to reach the end of the race and receive the heavenly prize for which God, through Christ Jesus, is calling us" (Philippians 3:14 NLT).

When you join the track team, for example, the work isn't done. Agreeing to run the hundred-meter dash isn't the equivalent of actually running the race. Getting in the blocks is only the beginning to blasting off and running the race. God's team is no different! Accepting Jesus as Lord and Savior is incredible, but we need to understand what it does—it puts us in the starting blocks. We agreed to stop running the race of life on our own, and we will now run it with Him. When the starter pistol sounds, signaling the start of the race, we cannot ignore it and stay in the blocks. No! That's doing nothing for His team. We must run the race.

Joining any team is not the same as playing on it. Again, I am not minimizing that first courageous step of joining God's team at all! Nothing can happen without that first step; it is a life-changing decision! However, after joining any team, you are expected to play in the games.

After signing my college scholarship, I didn't just place it in a glass picture frame and spend the rest of my life proudly gazing at my accomplishment. I knew that I was expected to prepare myself to go to college and play in the games. It is no different for Christians. After accepting Christ and joining His team, that's more of a reflection on the work of Christ. As for us? After saying yes to salvation, which results from all of Christ's work, our work has only begun.

Again, don't miss the point here. The God-ordained

work of a Christian begins after accepting Christ Jesus as our Lord and Savior. Jesus immediately wants to start the process of making new players ready to be useable in the game of life. He understands that we are excited, relieved, and joyful once we are accepted on His team. He loves that we are happy and full of joy, and the Bible says that all of heaven rejoices! However, He also knows that you're a new player and that He needs to prepare you for the game of life. We need to get into game shape! He knows the challenge that the opponent poses and wants to prepare us for battle!

I was extremely happy about my decision to join the Louisville Cardinals. While I did celebrate for many days and remained ecstatic about my accomplishment, I knew I had work to do on that football field at Louisville. And so I quickly began to get ready. It must be the same for newly signed Christians to God's team as well. Once we are saved and placed on the team, there is work to be done on the field of life. It is not the time to relax once you are saved. It is not the time to coast and get lazy. Once saved, we have signed up to spiritually get into the game of life, and so we must do everything we can to prepare to play.

Necessary Changes

To get me prepared to play for the Louisville Cardinals, preparatory changes had to be made. It was mutually understood that I could not plan on being a college success while depending on a high school skill set. My new team would require a new me. In much the same way, to effectively play on God's team requires a spiritually new me. Jesus requires all of His new players to make some necessary changes, which is why Paul reminds us, "Therefore, if anyone is in Christ, the new creation has come: The old has gone, the new is here!" (2 Corinthians 5:17).

The old must go. This change is what truly authenticates us as players on God's team. It's also what causes many would-be Christians to quit, because they do not want to change anything. But Jesus says that we must! The Holy Spirit must be allowed to change us from the inside out. These changes may not always be easy or comfortable, but they are absolutely necessary.

The apostle Paul is a great example of this—he knew that without spiritual transformation and a renewed perspective, there was no way he could effectively play on Jesus' team. Paul knew that if he remained in that "worst of sinners" condition that he would be of no use to God. So he let Jesus change him; it was required before Jesus could use him.

And it is no different with Christians today. We cannot resist change. If we are unwilling to let God remake us and prepare us to play on His team, then we are only holding ourselves back. It's understandable that due to years of familiarity and comfort with our former selves, we may struggle with letting the old ways go. But if we resist change, we will play horribly in the game of life. If we really knew how vital these spiritual changes were to our success as spiritual athletes on God's team, we would not be so resistant to them.

In 1 Corinthians 9:25, Paul says, "Everyone who competes in the games goes into strict training." He is absolutely right about that. Champion athletes of the world spend a lot of time making improvements, necessary changes, and working on anything that makes them better. For them, liking strict training is not the criteria used in deciding whether or not to do it. Instead, they only need one question answered: Will it help prepare me to win? If the answer is yes to that question, then that's the determining factor on whether or not they do it. Champions train hard—whether they like it or not—because they desire the beneficial results!

It must be no different for players on God's team! Christians may not always enjoy the strict spiritual training that playing for Christ requires, but just like champion athletes, we too must ask ourselves the more important question: Will letting Jesus change me prepare me to win the game of life? And the answer to that question is yes, it will. In fact, it guarantees a pleasing result. The writer of Hebrews notes, "No discipline seems pleasant at the time, but painful. Later on, however, it produces a harvest of righteousness and peace for those who have been trained by it" (Hebrews 12:11).

If you believe in God and have accepted Jesus Christ as your Lord and Savior, I am both happy and excited for you. But you must understand what you have done in making that decision. You have said to Jesus, "Coach, I believe in You and Your team, and I want to play on it." Jesus then says, "Welcome! I've been waiting for you! Now … let's get you ready to play."

⏱ TIME-OUT

I hope this session motivates you. I hope it informs you. I hope it makes it clear what it means to start being a Christian. Jesus saved you so that He could change you and then use you for His purposes. While there may be several changes that Jesus may need to make in your life, there are two we will zero in on in the next two sessions—strength and endurance. Satan likes to attack us in these areas, but Jesus knows how to get us ready to battle back and win. The key points in this seventh session are to first understand the necessity for change and then commit to letting it happen in our day-to-day lives.

⌘ DISCUSSION QUESTIONS

1. Since becoming a Christian, have you allowed Jesus to change you in any area that He wishes, or are you resistant to change? What changes are/were the hardest for you to accept?

2. What changes have you specifically experienced through Christ that has made you a better player on His team?

3. In what areas of your life is Jesus currently trying to change you? What are the current results?

4. In what ways are you completely different from when you first accepted Christ? What things have stayed the same?

5. Is there something that you honestly do not want to change, but know you must? What is it?

▶ WATCH THE WRAP-UP VIDEO

To watch the wrap-up video, go to www.tcstallings.com, and on the "Playing on God's Team" page, click "Wrap-Up Vids." Then watch the video entitled Sessions #5–7: The Recruitment Process.

STRENGTH TRAINING

I will never forget my first day of strength training as a collegiate athlete. To say it was a little different from my high school days would be an understatement. It was challenging, grueling, and even painful at times. But I pushed through the entire workout from start to finish; I kept completing these grueling sessions day after day. Many times I thought about quitting or skipping a session—but I didn't. Through faith in the coaches and the team's strengthening program, I was able to stick with the routine.

I ended each session exhausted and my entire body throbbed, but it was not long before I started to experience results from the training. When I first entered college, my bench press max was 175–200 pounds, and my power squat max was roughly 200–225 pounds. By the time I was a senior in college, however, these numbers increased to 410 pounds (for the bench press) and 585 pounds (for the power squat). These were the results of all those tough training sessions. The coaches added heavier weight each week, and I kept pushing.

The only things that would have prevented these fantastic strength gains were skipping workouts, holding back effort in the sessions, or quitting when the sessions got tough. That is why I tried to never miss a session, never train halfheartedly, and never reject the weight increases. I truly desired to keep getting stronger! And with persistence and faith in the plan, that is exactly what happened—I got much stronger.

My training caused my strength to go through the roof, which improved my physical health and appearance, and elevated the way I performed in the games. Eventually, my whole perspective toward training changed, going from having to, to wanting to. I had become willing to do anything the strength coaches asked me to do. I fully trusted them. It did not matter how much weight the coaches challenged me to lift—I knew they were skilled at creating training programs and would never put more weight on the bar than I could handle. They were always near whenever I trained, and they were always ready to help me if things ever got too tough.

The whole strength training system made me a much

better player. I knew that sticking with the team's strengthening program would only further my success. To be honest, I eventually looked forward to them because the results made the pain well worth the effort.

Strong Spiritual Muscles

As players on God's team, we too must spiritually strength train. Satan's team preys on the weak Christians, so Jesus tests our strength, assesses it, and strengthens us accordingly! We cannot reject His strength program, and we must be willing to complete the training He requires of us! Look at how James puts it:

> Consider it pure joy, my brothers and sisters, whenever you face trials of many kinds, because you know that the testing of your faith produces perseverance. Let perseverance finish its work so that you may be mature and complete, not lacking anything. (James 1:2–4)

The players on God's team are strong because Jesus is strong. What James is showing us here is how we do our part in developing His strength within us. What good is it to know that we have extreme power through Christ if we will not let Him train us to use it? We see in these verses that God's players must be willing to take on many kinds of trials and have a faithful attitude throughout the process. Although at times it can be difficult to push through trial after trial, we must trust the process, persevere, and finish the training. We must be willing to spiritually hit the gym. God wants to train us, but we have to be willing to train!

Trials can weigh us down at times; they can be tough. But pushing through these trials is our spiritual way of lifting weights! All of our problems, worries, doubts, fears, tests, and struggles can all serve as the heavy weight placed on the spiritual barbells of life. God calls us to trust the Holy Spirit to help us push through whatever amount of training God allows in our lives. This is the only way to grow and get stronger in our relationship with Him.

One More Rep! Push! C'mon!

We know what it's like to have our teammates push us, which is what James is doing in the scriptures quoted above. James encourages us to finish our tough training sessions and to stop always asking to be let out of them. If we quit training, then we quit growing. If growth is the goal, then don't shy away from the heavy weights, if that is what Jesus is giving to you. Trust the coach! Jesus will never give us more weight than we can handle (see 1 Corinthians 10:13). Regardless of the weight God chooses, we must trust Him and be willing to show up—and stay—for the duration of the session.

The Bible says that we can do all things through Christ who gives us strength (see Philippians 4:13). Let's apply this scripture correctly for once! Don't resist God's training by always asking for a way out of the tough trials. Instead, if He is training you, ask God to give you the grace to press through it. If God leaves that weight in your life, then beg Him for the power to push through so that your spiritual muscles continue to grow. When this happens regularly, our strength continues to mature and we become even greater players on God's team. Make it your goal today to become the strongest Christ follower you have ever been.

⏱ TIME-OUT

If you're anything like me, then I'm sure you do not like being weak in your sport. I am almost certain of that without ever having met you. I can't imagine anyone saying, "I am weak, and I'm proud of it. In fact, I plan to stay this way and win!" It just sounds completely ridiculous, right? Weaknesses on any team need to be dealt with. And your spiritual weaknesses are no different. You must be diligent about dealing with your weaknesses and allowing Christ to produce the power within you to overcome those weaknesses. Any good opponent will always attack your weaknesses consistently. So commit to getting spiritually stronger today.

🔡 DISCUSSION QUESTIONS

1. What are the weakest parts of your spiritual game? What are the strongest parts?

2. How do you address the weaker parts of your game to make you a stronger player for your sports team? What about God's team—how have you decided to address your spiritual weaknesses?

3. What ways are effective for training your spiritual muscles? How has Jesus been training you?

4. What's been the heaviest spiritual test/trial/struggle/ issue that you have had to face in your life? What was the result?

5. Do you consider yourself a strong Christian athlete? Why or why not? (Would your teammates agree with your answer?)

▶️ WATCH THE WRAP-UP VIDEO

To watch the wrap-up video, go to www.tcstallings.com, and on the "Playing on God's Team" page, click "Wrap-Up Vids." Then watch the video entitled Session #8: Strength Training.

ENDURANCE TRAINING

In 1 Corinthians 9:24–27, Paul uses the illustration of a determined runner running a race as a metaphor of living the Christian life. He writes:

> Do you not know that in a race all the runners run, but only one gets the prize? Run in such a way as to get the prize. Everyone who competes in the games goes into strict training. They do it to get a crown that will not last, but we do it to get a crown that will last forever. Therefore I do not run like someone running aimlessly; I do not fight like a boxer beating the air. No, I strike a blow to my body and make it my slave so that after I have preached to others, I myself will not be disqualified for the prize.

Let's go a little deeper with this illustration for a moment. Endurance is defined as "the capacity to keep going or to put up with pain for a long time."

Have you ever watched the Olympic Games? Maybe you are familiar with the 5,000-meter run. That's 12.5 laps around a regulation-sized track. Personally, I'm a huge fan of the sprints, but I cannot help but admire the endurance of the distance runners. They just go … and go … and go. If the runners start to get sore, or mentally feel like giving up, they usually do not quit. They know that they can't stop if they want the victory. The prize is not at the 3,000-meter mark or even the 4,999-meter mark. No, the victory is at the finish line! Quitting at any point before reaching the finish line is a decision to lose.

There are many things that affect an athlete's decision to endure a tough situation or give up. Pain is definitely a challenge for endurance, and health is another. Fear can also be a hindrance for those wanting to push through. While some athletes choose to quit, others rise up and turn in epic performances.

How do certain athletes have what it takes to endure under such uncomfortable conditions while others do not? Some athletes can do this because they endurance train regularly. Endurance training helps us to never be so broken by the rigors of the sport that we can't press on. The goal of developing endurance is simple: it is so that we will never have to give up or quit short of victory.

When it comes to the way we endure for our sports teams, Paul says, "They do it to get a crown that will not last, but we do it to get a crown that will last forever" (1 Corinthians 9:25). What do they do to receive a crown that doesn't last? They endure the training. He then says that players on Team Jesus should endure strict training because our prize is much greater.

Paul is speaking here from an eternal perspective. It's a quick reminder as to why we chose to accept a spot on God's team in the first place. Eternal salvation! If motivation is said to be one of the keys to endurance, then eternity with Christ should provide Christians with an unlimited supply of it.

Paul reminds us of what happens when God's team endures and we stick with the game plan: "Let us not become weary in doing good, for at the proper time we will reap a harvest if we do not give up" (Galatians 6:9). And James tells us more about receiving the ultimate prize when the final whistle blows: "Blessed is the one who perseveres under trial because, having stood the test, that person will receive the crown of life that the Lord has promised to those who love him" (James 1:12).

But It Hurts

While playing on God's team, we will definitely have our share of pain. He said, "In this life you will have trouble. But take heart! I have overcome the world" (John 16:33). Jesus promises that there will be moments that will require great endurance. Life will certainly require us to play a few games in pain, but when we take time to reflect on God's mercy, grace, and sacrificial love for us, then we should be more than motivated to endure a few trials in life for Him!

Whenever we feel like quitting, we need to set our sights on Jesus Christ, who is the ultimate example of endurance. After being beaten and nailed to the cross, Jesus hung in there for us. He was committed to His purpose and accepted the call to endure pain and suffering. We know that Jesus thought about quitting. He actually prayed for God to remove Him from the responsibility of dying if it were possible (see Luke 22:42). But motivated by God's plan and His love for you and for me, Jesus prayed for the Father's will to be done, not His own will.

Jesus' desire to quit was overpowered by His desire to endure! The temptation to give up was overcome by the desire to press on and do the will of His Father! His hate for the pain was trumped by His love for you and for me! Jesus had every right to walk away; He was God. However, the only giving up He did was giving up His spirit to death.

Ironically, this one death gave the whole world an opportunity to experience true life.

Jesus definitely endured. And we benefited from it.

Now it's your turn, when called upon, to endure for Him.

⏱ TIME-OUT

Our coaches never want us to quit. They try and tough it out of us, yell it out of us, and even scare it out of us at times. Why do they do this? It is because quitting is the last thing they want us to do. My high school coach is still my all-time favorite coach. I'd never quit on him. Never. But do you know what? He didn't die for me so that I can have eternal life. But Jesus did—my spiritual head coach. There is no way you or I should ever give any coach or team more effort toward endurance than what Jesus gets from us. Never.

⚏ DISCUSSION QUESTIONS

1. As a Christian, what types of trials or temptations have made you feel like giving in?

2. What is the hardest thing you have ever had to spiritually endure? What was the result?

3. Is there anything that you feel "has your number" spiritually—meaning you can never seem to endure through it?

4. What types of situations in your life weaken your ability to endure? How have you addressed these obstacles?

WATCH THE WRAP-UP VIDEO

To watch the wrap-up video, go to www.tcstallings.com, and on the "Playing on God's Team" page, click "Wrap-Up Vids." Then watch the video entitled Session #9: Endurance Training.

THE PLAYBOOK

On September 2, 2000, I found myself at starting tailback in the biggest game of my collegiate career—Louisville vs. Kentucky. The game ended with my overtime game-winning touchdown run after taking the handoff on a play called "Ace Right, 24 Counter." It's one of my all-time favorite moments. But here's a question for you: What would have happened had I not known what "Ace Right, 24 Counter" was when the play call came into the huddle? What if I had not studied my playbook? What if I thought I knew it, but really I had it confused with another play? If I had not known what the playbook said to do concerning this play, my actions would have not resulted in that game-winning touchdown run.

Players are without excuse when it comes to knowing the plays, especially since they have unlimited access to the playbook. I've been on teams with players who would hit the playing field without knowing the plays, which would really frustrate the coaches because not knowing the playbook always crippled even the best of players. It also hurt the entire team, since each play requires a collective unified effort. Poor playbook knowledge breaks the line of communication between the coach and player during games because they are not on the same page. Players who show a severe lack of playbook knowledge are quickly removed from the game and harshly reminded that if they do not know the plays, then they cannot be used.

The same responsibility exists for players on God's team as well. His players must study their playbooks. Paul put it this way: "All Scripture is God-breathed and is useful for teaching, rebuking, correcting and training in righteousness, so that the servant of God may be thoroughly equipped for every good work" (2 Timothy 3:16–17).

As players on God's team, our spiritual playbook is the Bible. We all know it is a pretty big book, but so are the playbooks on most athletic teams. And so are the business manuals, company handbooks, and college textbooks we have to read too. We readily read these big books because the knowledge inside helps produce the touchdowns, the big raises, the promotions, and the prestigious degrees. Even if we complain about how long the book is or how many chapters we have to complete, we usually suck it up and get the job done because it pays off in the end. It's no different in the spiritual game of life. If you want to play effectively on God's team, then you must study the plays!

There is absolutely no other way to play for God than to know and follow the Bible. If we have not studied God's Word, then we simply will not know what to do. This usually leads to confusion on our part, which then leads to the dangerous practice of spiritual improvisation. We depend solely on common sense alone, and so basically we wing it. We trade in studying the playbook for human logic, personal opinions, the advice of friends, as well as other sources. And as a result, we end up making the wrong choice in the game of life that only leads to stumble after stumble.

While some stumbling is inevitable throughout our lives, our playbook—if regularly studied—offers a solution: "The LORD makes firm the steps of the one who delights in him; though he may stumble, he will not fall, for the LORD upholds him with his hand" (Psalm 37:23–24). And one of the ways to "delight in him" is to study His Word. The psalmist says that the blessed person is the one,

> Whose delight is in the law of the LORD,
> and who meditates on his law day and night.

That person is like a tree planted by streams of water,
which yields its fruit in season
and whose leaf does not wither—
whatever they do prospers. (Psalm 1:2–3)

Our playbook is our scriptural guide. It is our most reliable source of direction. It is our playbook for the game of life! Sure, the Holy Spirit is inside of us to provide guidance along the way, but guidance toward what? He provides us guidance toward execution of the playbook.

We should constantly study our playbook and be determined to keep growing in knowledge of it. Sure, we will have some close calls in the game of life, but we can find comfort in knowing that Jesus is always watching and coaching, and He knows the right plays to call. But for any of this to benefit us in the game of life, and for us to be useable players on God's team, we must regularly read, study, and internalize our spiritual playbook—the Bible.

⏱ TIME-OUT

You know what's funny about all of this? When I played in college, you know what they called our playbook? They called our playbook the Bible. In the pros you know what they called it? Yep—the Bible. They'd say, "You better treat this like the Bible, son." Even the world unintentionally knows how important the

Bible is supposed to be to God's team. On our sports teams, we stay in our playbooks to give ourselves the best chance in the game. On God's team, we must commit to doing the same in the game of life. And we need to do this daily, because most sports have a game or two per week—but God's team plays the game of life every day.

🖳 DISCUSSION QUESTIONS

1. Do you read the Bible every day? If not, what prevents you from doing so?

2. Has there ever been a time when knowing Scripture helped you? What about a time when not knowing Scripture has hurt you?

3. Share with the group your daily Bible study routine.

📺 WATCH THE WRAP-UP VIDEO

To watch the wrap-up video, go to www.tcstallings.com, and on the "Playing on God's Team" page, click "Wrap-Up Vids." Then watch the video entitled Session #10: The Playbook.

STUDY
THE OPPONENT

In any game, in any battle, and in any competition, it is crucial to know exactly what or who you are facing. It is never good to not know what you are truly up against. Many battles are lost before the game is ever played due to the unfamiliarity of the opponent. This is why most teams spend hours studying the opponent before a game ever begins. The more they know about the opponent, the less likely they are to be out-smarted by them.

When I played football, each player would always receive the weekly "scouting report." This report, which contained the results from weeks of studying and evaluations, contained valuable information and accurately told us everything we needed to know about the team we would soon face. It even informed us about that team's head coach and his play calling tendencies. We were also required to sit and watch film, which were previously recorded games involving our opponent. By reading the scouting report and watching the opponent in action against other teams, we became familiar with the players, their coach, and their schemes.

Players on God's team must study the opponent as well if we are to win at the game of life. We have not talked much about our opponent yet, but he is crafty and committed to his plans. I am, of course, speaking of Satan and his demons. In our playbooks, we'll see a "spiritual scouting report" designed to familiarize us with what we are sure to face when it comes to Satan and his team. Here is some of that report: "Be alert and of sober mind. Your enemy the devil prowls around like a roaring lion looking for someone to devour" (1 Peter 5:8).

We can look at this part of the scouting report and instantly learn a few things about Satan. We can see how we make ourselves vulnerable to his attacks when our minds are not where they should be. We can also see that Satan is a prowler, much like a lion. This is valuable information, for it exposes one of his most successful methods of attack—the art of stealth and deception.

Have you ever seen a lion hunt? Does it just pounce on the scene, roaring loudly, announcing its attack beforehand? Of course it doesn't. Rather, it crouches low and gets in stealth mode, hidden from view, inching along the fields of grass, quietly stalking its prey. And then it patiently waits for the opportune moment to devour its unsuspecting prey. Satan loves to attack us when we least expect it, which is why Peter admonishes us to stay alert.

Watching film not only had to do with watching an upcoming opponent, but we also had to take a look at our own previously played games. This was a great way to catch costly personal mistakes that were made so that we would not repeat them. We need to do the same thing by recalling previous "us versus Satan" moments. You can do this by simply replaying a time in your life when you let Satan get the best of you. How did he sneak up on you? At what moment did he take control? What methods did he use? What godly methods did you fail to use? Why weren't you victorious? What must you do differently to win next time?

Identifying how Satan attacked you in past situations will help prepare you for future ones. You can also revisit times in which you defeated him and make mental notes of the strategies that brought success.

Satan is a serious evil competitor that we cannot take lightly. Not understanding who we are dealing with when it comes to Satan is a loss waiting to happen. I don't want to paint a picture of fear because we are not to be afraid of him, but what I am asking you to do is to be aware of him. Be prepared. Respect your opponent and humbly ask God to keep you focused. Never forget what the battle is really all about, and whom the war is actually against.

The truth is that we have a tendency to focus on fighting people when the war is really spiritual. Paul reminds us of this when he writes, "For our struggle is not against flesh and blood, but against the rulers, against the authorities, against the powers of this dark world and against the spiritual forces of evil in the heavenly realms" (Ephesians 6:12).

This describes the spiritually evil and powerful team that all Christians face. While earthly "flesh and blood" athletes compete on grass fields, wooden courts, pools, tracks, and arenas, God's team battles on a spiritual field of play. This is why we need to give daily attention to our spiritual development, never forgetting the type of fight we are in. Satan knows that the game of life is spiritual, and he will easily exploit the weaknesses of those who do not understand this. On the other hand, if we know the opponent and know the nature of the battle while following our coach, we are assured spiritual victory in the game of life.

I love how James shares God's game plan with us concerning Satan: "'God opposes the proud, but shows favor to the humble.' Submit yourselves, then, to God. Resist the devil, and he will flee from you" (James 4:6–7). Do you believe this part of God's plan? If you are humble, and if you submit to God, then you will overpower Satan and he will run from you. You were not designed to keep losing to

Satan. Don't ever give in to that kind of thinking concerning sin! Resist the devil by staying committed to Jesus and His team … and he will flee. Picture *that!*

⏱ TIME-OUT

It's uncomfortable to know that there is an evil force constantly attacking our lives. But isn't it comforting to know that Jesus has a plan that, when executed, defeats it? If we know what the Bible says about how to resist Satan, we can put it into action, protect ourselves from his evil game plan of destruction, and play the game of life confidently—not fearfully.

🔲 DISCUSSION QUESTIONS

1. What does it look like for Satan to attack you spiritually? In what ways can you recognize these attacks?

2. In what ways can you keep from becoming an "easy target" for the enemy?

3. Discuss Ephesians 6:12, which talks about the type of battle we are fighting. What does this mean to you?

▶ WATCH THE WRAP-UP VIDEO

To watch the wrap-up video, go to www.tcstallings.com, and on the "Playing on God's Team" page, click "Wrap-Up Vids." Then watch the video entitled Session #11: Studying the Opponent.

PRACTICE

Every day of the year, you can bet that some team, somewhere, is practicing. This is the one part of sports that should be no surprise to anyone. There isn't a person in the world aspiring to join a team who does not expect to have some sort of practice before actually playing a game. Anything we desire to become skilled at doing will require some version of practice.

We all know what the results of practicing are—we tend to get better! We perform better and our overall effectiveness increases. We are more successful as a team because we have taken pride in striving for perfection. Sure, nobody is perfect, but the team closest to it will have reached its full potential. I love the idea of being the best, so practice (for the most part) was a joy for me.

However, there were a few rare times where I did not

want to practice. The times I dreaded practicing usually had nothing to do with the sport itself. Instead, it would usually be things like extremely cold weather or rain that would kill my excitement about practicing. If not poor weather, then it would be fatigue from a lack of sleep, or my aching body due to weight training that made me want to skip practice. Whatever the reason, there were certainly days where I didn't want to do it.

I would never follow through on the idea of missing practice because our coaches had a little rule that discouraged most players from missing a session: "If you don't practice, you don't play." There were basically two reasons for this firm rule. Players who missed practices would have no idea what to do in the actual game, and the other problem was that without daily practice, a player gets worse, not better.

God's team is absolutely no different, and it requires that players practice daily. If we do not practice living out Scripture in our lives, then we should not expect to perform well in the game of life! This is how Jesus put it: "But the one who hears my words and does not put them into practice is like a man who built a house on the ground without a foundation. The moment the torrent struck that house, it collapsed and its destruction was complete" (Luke 6:49).

Just as you will limit your effectiveness by missing practice in your particular sport, the same holds true for God's team. We hold ourselves back from succeeding in the game of life. Even if we know the spiritual playbook, it's useless if we refuse to practice the plays within it! We all have experienced this at times, haven't we? We've all at one time known exactly what to do in a spiritually tempting situation but simply didn't put what we knew into practice. Jesus called the right play, and the Holy Spirit was ready to lead us in executing it, but we ignored the play call. We refused to put the play into practice, and the result was usually sin and guilt.

Remember Luke 6:49 when you are tempted to skip putting the Word of God into practice. This bad habit only does one thing: it puts us on the path of collapse and complete destruction when we face trials and opposition.

Jesus Christ, our spiritual head coach, always practiced hard when He played the game of life here on earth. We have our earthly sports role models, but Jesus is the best role model for players on His team. He practiced what He preached, and He practiced what He knew about God's Word. To the players on His team who believe in the way He played the game of life, Jesus has a message: "Very truly I tell you, whoever believes in me will do the works I have been doing" (John 14:12).

He said it plainly. To play like Christ, we must practice like Christ.

⏱ TIME-OUT

As an athlete, I am hoping that no one needs to convince you that practice is important. As a Christian athlete, you play on two teams—your sports team and Team Jesus. You must never slack on practicing for either one. The problem is that God's team usually gets the short end of the stick, and we all know that won't work. So resolve today to work hard at putting God's Word into practice each and every day.

▦ DISCUSSION QUESTIONS

1. Name something you were doing wrong or couldn't achieve concerning your sport but practiced hard enough until you got it right. What motivated you to keep at it?

2. What scriptures and spiritual concepts—if any—do you have trouble obeying or putting into practice?

3. What would you say is the most motivating reasons to practice at executing Scripture properly?

▶ WATCH THE WRAP-UP VIDEO

To watch the wrap-up video, go to www.tcstallings.com, and on the "Playing on God's Team" page, click "Wrap-Up Vids." Then watch the video entitled Session #12: Practice.

TEAM MEETINGS

Like most head coaches who require regular meetings with their players, Jesus requires His players to attend His team meetings as well. We are strongly encouraged to regularly fellowship with other Christians. Hebrews tells us:

> And let us consider how we may spur one another on toward love and good deeds, not giving up meeting together, as some are in the habit of doing, but encouraging one another—and all the more as you see the Day approaching. (Hebrews 10:24–25)

God's team holds team meetings in the form of church services, Bible study groups, mission trips, community service projects, retreats, and much more. Any time bodies of true believers come together in spirit and in truth for a God-honoring purpose, then that's a team meeting.

I realize that when the subject of going to church comes up, things can get touchy. That is because attending church is a heavily opinionated subject in our day and age. It is my desire that we do our very best to consider only Scripture (not our opinions) when approaching this topic. And it is important to always remember that the church is the people on God's team, not the building in which His team meets.

When the Bible says that we should not give up meeting together as some of us are in the habit of doing, something immediately jumps out at me. It's the words *give up*. Hebrews clearly encourages us to meet with other believers and to not give up on seeking out a church—a body of Christ followers—that honors God. It does not matter where the church meets. If your church family meets in a building or in a home, then that is where you need to go. If your church family meets in a tent, then that is where you need to be. The location of the meeting facility may be different for different groups of people, and that is perfectly fine. But no matter what, we all should pray for guidance on choosing a church family that is near us, and meeting regularly with our teammates should be taken seriously.

On your sports team, you most likely have a regularly scheduled full team meeting, and then there are the smaller and more intimate position meetings. These are always a top priority—they are never optional. On God's team, our team meetings must be a top priority as well—they are not optional. Whether it be the church services, prayer meetings, mission trips, Sunday school classes, midweek Bible studies, men's or women's retreats, or home groups that meet regularly to study Scripture, the point is that Jesus wants His players to regularly meet with Him as a team!

The Bible, which is God's game plan for life, commands us to regularly come together as a team to learn about Him, honor Him, and worship Him and, at the same time, encourage one another in the game of life. This is meant to be obeyed. The truth is that we need each other to walk out our faith. There is a desperate need for spiritual accountability and encouragement among Christians today. When we meet as a spiritual team, we can encourage one another to keep pressing forward and remind one another that no one has to play this difficult game of life alone.

There is an old example that illustrates this well. You can take a single pencil and snap it in half, which is easily done when it is just one pencil. But if you try to do the same thing with a bundle of pencils tied together, then it is suddenly not so easy anymore, right? The pencils are unified; the bundle is too strong to break. Together, it is almost impossible to snap any of them. Likewise, a solo Christian who resorts to playing in the game of life alone is not as strong as a team of true, unified, and committed followers of Jesus. Together, and behind Christ's leadership, Satan is facing a team that will not break.

⏱ TIME-OUT

If you currently do not have a regular opportunity to meet with other true Christians, now is a great time to stop and ask Jesus to place you in the one He wants for you, in His timing. Make this a priority in your life.

▦ DISCUSSION QUESTIONS

1. What kinds of things do you think of when you hear the word *church*?

2. Why do you think some Christians give up meeting together?

3. What are the greatest benefits you have experienced from meeting with other Christians?

4. If you were to regularly skip team and/or position meetings for your sport, what important information might you miss out on? How would that affect your success as a player?

▶ WATCH THE WRAP-UP VIDEO

To watch the wrap-up video, go to www.tcstallings.com, and on the "Playing on God's Team" page, click "Wrap-Up Vids." Then watch the video entitled Session #13: Team Meetings.

THE OPEN DOOR POLICY

My college coach would always tell us, "If any of you ever need to talk to me about anything, then feel free to come and see me at any time. I have an open door policy." This policy was important to him because it gave players the permission to come into his office at any time and discuss anything. He hated it when players were having a problem but chose not to use his offer to talk to him about it. I suppose he felt unappreciated. Maybe. Or maybe some of us didn't understand the true value of having a coach who was willing to take the time to listen, process, and address our concerns. This is the same problem that happens with some players on God's team too.

Jesus has also instituted an open door policy for His players. It is called prayer. Our spiritual head coach always has the door open and expects to hear from us regularly.

And this open door is not only open at breakfast or dinner, before traveling, before going to bed, or most other habitual times that are normally reserved for prayer. Instead, the door is always open, which is why the Bible tells us to constantly remain in a prayerful mind-set about all things. Take a look at one of the shortest yet most precise commands in the Bible: "Pray continually" (1 Thessalonians 5:17).

The idea here is that we remain prayer ready at all times. Our spiritual head coach wants to be continually involved in every moment of the game! And so the door is always open for us to have a talk with God, and we can talk about anything—even the little things that we think He doesn't care about. There is no prayer that is too small!

Have you ever heard the saying, "Just a little spark can cause a forest fire"? It's true when it comes to sin, problems, concerns, and decisions. Little issues can easily grow into big ones if they are not quickly addressed. Jesus wants to address our little sparks too, which can prevent bigger spiritual fires in our lives.

In college, some players ran into problems that appeared too big, complex, or personal for even the head coach to handle. That's understandable—maybe they were too big. With Jesus, however, the issues are never too big, and He has a remedy for any problem the game of life brings. It does not make much sense to withhold our spiritual problems from the One who has the guaranteed ability to solve them! Yet we still manage to do this at times. But if we commit to praying about our problems when they arise, then we are guaranteed His relief! God has promised to respond to our calls to Him with tremendous love and care.

The Psalms encourage us in this area of giving all of our problems to Jesus because He truly does care about us. The psalmist declared:

> Cast your cares on the LORD
> and he will sustain you;
> he will never let
> the righteous be shaken. (Psalm 55:22)

Not only are we promised a solution when we cast our cares on Him, but we are also guaranteed that His solution will work. In fact, Jesus wants to hear our concerns. Just look at how the Lord shows His compassion in 1 Peter 5:7: "Cast all your anxiety on him because he cares for you."

Jesus knows that His spiritual athletes will deal with all kinds of issues in the game. And so He wants His players to go into the game with a sense of peace! Worrying about our problems all of the time leads to awful execution of God's game plan. On God's team, however, if we continuously find ourselves performing poorly due to stress, fear, uncertainty, anxiety, and confusion, then we can be certain that the open door policy of Jesus is not being used. In God's game plan, He assures us that He does not create these kinds of emotions in us, but instead promises us a spirit of "power, love and self-discipline" (2 Timothy 1:7). He can eliminate anything that hinders us from giving Him our best—if we trust Him, pray, and ask for it in faith! Continual prayer displays continual trust and faith in God, and our spiritual head coach absolutely loves this from His players.

The blessing of being able to speak humbly and directly to the God of the universe through Jesus is often overlooked, underused, and undervalued. What is worse is that, for many, prayer is often a last resort. Have you ever heard someone say, "Oh well, I guess all I can do now is just pray" (which usually suggests that prayer has become an option only after trying several other solutions first)? This is out of order. Jesus already knows the solutions to all of our problems, so instead of leading with action and then praying that it works, why not lead with prayer to begin with so that we can then take action that will work? On God's team, prayer must be the first option, not the backup plan.

Do you remember Psalm 139:16, where God declares to have ordained our days before any one of them came to be? It's crazy to not consult the One who wrote out our entire lives and scripted His own awesome plan for them! We are encouraged to make prayer a priority each day: "And we are confident that he hears us whenever we ask for anything that pleases him. And since we know he hears us when we make our requests, we also know that he will give us what we ask for" (1 John 5:14–15 NLT).

Our spiritual head coach loves answering the humble prayers of His players, as we ask for His will to be done on earth as it is in heaven! That is why His door is always open.

⏱ TIME-OUT

I hope one thing is clear from this session: You cannot play on God's team if prayer is not on your "must do daily" list. Understanding that Jesus uses your prayers in the process of coaching you through life should motivate you to not slack in this area. You will get crushed in the game of life if you do not pray when you play. And we play every day, all day long. So when should we pray? Continually.

🗩 DISCUSSION QUESTIONS

1. Describe your prayer relationship with Jesus. (How often do you pray? What do you usually pray about?)

2. Do you have a prayer strategy? Share it with the others in the group.

3. What are some of your favorite answered prayers?

4. Has there ever been a time in which you struggled to pray about something? What was it, and what made it hard to pray about?

▶ WATCH THE WRAP-UP VIDEO

To watch the wrap-up video, go to www.tcstallings.com, and on the "Playing on God's Team" page, click "Wrap-Up Vids." Then watch the video entitled Session #14: Open Door Policy.

THE UNIFORM

During any sports game, how can you tell the difference between the two teams? Their uniforms easily solve this problem. The distinct colors, styles, names, logos, and numbers of a team uniform make it easy to tell one team apart from the other. Two of the main purposes for uniforms are identification and protection.

With God's team, this is no different. We have a spiritual uniform that serves these same purposes of identification and protection. Unlike the sports uniforms that feature jerseys, padding, and logos, the Christian uniform is spiritual, protecting and identifying us as spiritual players on God's team. Paul reminds of this in Ephesians: "For our struggle is not against flesh and blood, but against the rulers, against the authorities, against the powers of this dark world and against the spiritual forces of evil in the heavenly realms" (Ephesians 6:12).

This scripture is so important for us to understand as players on Team Jesus, because it stresses the spirituality of the fight—not the physicality, which usually gets the most attention. Let's take sexual immorality, for example. This sin has to be fought spiritually, not just physically. The physical sin of sexual immorality usually originates with the spiritual sin nature of lust and the spiritual temptation from Satan to act on that lust. This is why our spiritual uniform is important—it is designed for the type of game we play.

A Uniform Identifies

Let's take a look at our spiritual uniform, starting with the parts of it that serve the purpose of identification. Earlier we said that uniforms identify and help distinguish competing teams. Jesus' team looks totally different than Satan's team, which means there should be no confusion when these two teams compete. (Can people tell which spiritual team you play for?)

The Bible describes the identity of both teams. Let's take a look at each team's spiritual identification. Satan's team has certain characteristics and attributes that identify it. Paul writes about these in Galatians 5:19–21 (NLT):

When you follow the desires of your sinful nature, the results are very clear: sexual immorality, impurity,

lustful pleasures, idolatry, sorcery, hostility, quar-
reling, jealousy, outbursts of anger, selfish ambition,
dissension, division, envy, drunkenness, wild parties,
and other sins like these. Let me tell you again, as I
have before, that anyone living that sort of life will
not inherit the Kingdom of God.

But God's team has a different set of attributes alto-
gether. In the very next verses Paul goes on to write:

But the Holy Spirit produces this kind of fruit in our
lives: love, joy, peace, patience, kindness, goodness,
faithfulness, gentleness, and self-control. There is no
law against these things! (Galatians 5:22–23 NLT)

The choices Christians make play a strong role in the
way onlookers perceive our faith and our team. This is the
part of our spiritual uniform—our actions—that identifies us
with Christ! Galatians 5:22–23 paints a clear picture of what
our spiritual uniform should look like as followers of Christ.
Through the process of letting the Holy Spirit continually
make us better players, we will live by the fruit of His Spirit,
and it will be evident to the world that we belong to God's
team. The bottom line is that, in the eyes of our audience, our
actions clearly identify us with either Jesus or Satan.

A Uniform Protects

Let's take a look at another function of a uniform, which serves the purpose of protection. Like the helmet of a hockey player or the mouth guard of a boxer, there are parts of our uniform that keep us from getting injured. On God's team, we too must put on the parts of our uniform that spiritually protect us from injury. The Bible calls this the armor of God, which is found in Ephesians 6:14–18:

> Stand firm then, with the belt of truth buckled around your waist, with the breastplate of righteousness in place, and with your feet fitted with the readiness that comes from the gospel of peace. In addition to all this, take up the shield of faith, with which you can extinguish all the flaming arrows of the evil one. Take the helmet of salvation and the sword of the Spirit, which is the word of God.
>
> And pray in the Spirit on all occasions with all kinds of prayers and requests. (Ephesians 6:14–18)

Whenever I read these verses, I am reminded of when the equipment managers on my football team would pass out uniforms. They would warn us to wear every piece when we played so that we would not get injured and regret it later. This same advice should be taken by players on

God's team concerning the protective portion of our spiritual uniform. Each piece of our uniform is important! We will surely regret leaving any part of the uniform behind when we take on Satan each day!

⏱ TIME-OUT

I'd say that by now you can clearly see that being on God's team is not just a matter of claiming membership, but also looking the part. This means that we are spiritually led in our actions and spiritually prepared to fight sin.

⛶ DISCUSSION QUESTIONS

1. How does it make you feel to know that what you do in life while wearing the team name can positively or negatively affect others' perceptions of Christ?

2. From knowing you, what have people learned about Jesus? About being a Christian?

3. What do you think it means to live like a Christian? Look like a Christian? How about to talk like a Christian?

▶ WATCH THE WRAP-UP VIDEO

To watch the wrap-up Video, go to www.tcstallings.com, and on the "Playing on God's Team" page, click "Wrap-Up Vids." Then watch the video entitled Session #15: The Uniform.

THE ARMOR OF GOD

As we discussed in the last session, Ephesians 6:14–18 tells us about our spiritual uniform that we are to wear as members of God's team. Since each piece of the uniform is important, it is vital that we take a look at all of the pieces, beginning with the belt of truth.

The Belt

Paul writes, "Stand firm then, with the belt of truth buckled around your waist" (Ephesians 6:14).

What does the belt in your closet do? For starters, it keeps your pants from falling down. For me as a football player, a dysfunctional belt could cause all sorts of other problems. Even the biggest, fastest, and most talented players would have trouble maneuvering around the field if their pants were sliding down their legs. At first thought, a belt doesn't seem like much in the overall uniform, but that little piece of equipment has a big job.

The belt of truth in our spiritual uniform handles the task of holding everything up and together. The focus here is on living a life that is based on God's truth, the truth that Jesus is who He says He is and will do everything He said He would for His team. Belief in this truth will always hold us up and keep us together, even in the midst of the game of life.

We can add to this the call to always speak the truth, and avoid saying one thing but living a life that says something completely different (which is called hypocrisy). We can't claim that Jesus is the truth and then not follow this truth ourselves! We cannot be liars. Manipulators. Deceivers. We cannot be "Scripture twisters" (knowingly bending the truth of Scripture to fit our personal agendas). Since we know the truth, we need to live lives that are held together by the truth of Jesus Christ alone. Without the belt of truth firmly in place, our lives will eventually fall apart and come crumbling down.

The Breastplate

Paul mentions next the "breastplate of righteousness" (Ephesians 6:14).

In football, our breastplate is attached to our shoulder pads. It protects our sternum, heart, and chest cavity from the hits we take on the field. It also protects parts of our ribs from being broken and potentially puncturing other sensitive organs. The main function of the breastplate is to protect the vital (most important) organs of a player. If left unprotected, a blow to these vital organs could lead to paralysis and even death. With our spiritual uniform, the spiritual breastplate of righteousness serves a similar purpose—it protects the vital parts of our faith.

It is called the breastplate of *righteousness*. A Christian's conduct is the number one indicator of the presence or absence of God in his or her life. We can't freely live a worldly life and still play on God's team! Christians must be as righteous as the plan of God will allow them to be. This righteousness does not amount to a perfect life; instead, it is a life viewed as righteous because of the relationship we have through Christ. Through a commitment to true repentance, continually turning from sin, and the regular refining of our lives by the Holy Spirit, we can live a life that displays the righteousness necessary to play on God's team.

(I want to encourage everyone to take moment and read Ezekiel 18:20–32 to hear an informative message from God concerning the vitality of our righteousness.)

The Footwear

After the breastplate of righteousness, Paul says that our feet should be "fitted with the readiness that comes from the gospel of peace" (Ephesians 6:15).

In most sports, a specific type of shoe must be worn. For football, each player always wears some type of cleat. Slipping is a part of the game, and without cleated shoes a player is destined to slip and fall. Players with cleats have more control and traction during games. Come rain, sleet, or snow, with my cleated shoes firmly on my feet, I was able to play hard and fast, without the fear of falling. If the opposite were true of my footwear, then I would have played nervous, unsure, and hesitant—while definitely slipping and falling all over the field.

In a similar way, players on God's team must also have the proper footwear. The focus of Scripture here is on the readiness and peace that stems from our confidence in the gospel of Jesus Christ.

We need to be 100 percent confident in His game plan. Spiritual confidence through knowing the truth of God's Word produces a peace no one can comprehend (see Philippians 4:6–7). This same peace helps us to continually trust in God's plan and remain confident in it. If we are doubtful or unsure of the truth of God's Word, or if we are unstable when it comes to our complete trust in Scripture, then our footing is not firm. We then open ourselves up to the possibility of falling for all sorts of spiritual untruths, Scripture twists, and biblical distortions. This is what it looks like to spiritually slip on the field of play.

Just as there are many weather climates that will challenge an athlete's traction, so there are many religions, doctrines, opinions, and theories that will challenge the traction of spiritual athletes on God's team. Christians must be rooted and firmly grounded in the Word of God so that we can make spiritually sure-footed moves in the game of life.

The Shield

Paul continues, "In addition to all this, take up the shield of faith, with which you can extinguish all the flaming arrows of the evil one" (Ephesians 6:16).

As a running back, I depended on my offensive line to block for me whenever I ran with the ball. The plays were designed to work best if I followed the big guys. But there were times when a play was designed to go right and I would decide to cut back and take it to the left. I'd make a few moves, look good for a moment, then get crushed by seven or eight unblocked players. Why would I run opposite of the blocking? Well, it was usually because I would put too much faith in my own abilities and foolishly try to go my own way. Other times, however, I thought I knew better than the play that was called in the huddle. Needless to say, my head coach did not appreciate the lack of faith in the scheme—and neither did my offensive line. Abandoning the plan and losing faith in the blocking hurt the whole team.

Being on God's team, we have a strong shield of protection. The shield that we have as part of our armor is the shield of *faith*. Faith in God, His plan, His Son, His gospel, His promises, His truth, and the power of His Spirit all combine to produce a great shield! This protects us from Satan, his attacks, his schemes, and his team. Without faith to stand behind, it is impossible to be a player with whom God is pleased (see Hebrews 11:6).

Faith is what keeps us playing when the game gets extremely rough, violent, confusing, scary, or even challenging. When we begin to lose faith in something, it becomes easier to come out from behind the protection of it. This is dangerous living for those playing on God's team. We can't take on Satan without Jesus leading the way. In John 15:5 (NLT), Jesus says it plainly: "Yes, I am the vine; you are the branches. Those who remain in me, and I in them, will produce much fruit. For apart from me you can do nothing."

Whenever we lose faith in Jesus concerning any situation, and head in another direction, we are saying that we think we can handle it better and without His help. This is nothing more than trading a secure situation for an unsecure one. Whenever we are tempted to lose faith in the timing and purposes of Jesus, all we need to do is open our Bibles and read Proverbs 20:24: "A person's steps are directed by the LORD. How then can anyone understand their own way?"

⏱ TIME-OUT

This session covered a few key concepts, centering around being honest and truthful, showing that you have the power to live a life apart from sinning deliberately and that you can keep faith in God's plan—and you can maintain this throughout your entire life. If you think this is a lot, I completely understand. I used to think that way too; that is, until I looked at all the different sacrifices, commitments, and disciplines that football consistently required of me. And I had no problem complying. So I asked myself, "After all I give to football, how much more should I be willing to give God's team?"

⚏ DISCUSSION QUESTIONS

1. How would you describe what it means to live a life that is held together by the truth of Jesus Christ?

2. Describe your level of confidence in the Bible and what you have been taught about your faith so far. Is there anything you struggle to truly believe? Have you asked

Jesus for clarity regarding that struggle? (Remember that He has an open door policy!)

3. What do you think of when you hear the word *righteous*? What's the difference between righteous living and perfect living?

4. Describe a time when your faith was weak and you had trouble trusting Jesus. What happened as a result? Did you stay the course or go your own way?

▶ WATCH THE WRAP-UP VIDEO

The next wrap-up video covers both Sessions 16 and 17, and it will take place after Session 17.

THE ARMOR OF GOD: THE HELMET

As part of putting on our spiritual armor, Paul instructs us to "take the helmet of salvation" (Ephesians 6:17). I'm sure I don't have to convince anyone of the importance of the helmet for any sport or activity that requires the use of one. What does a helmet do? Why it protects a person's head, of course.

Are you familiar with the term *concussion*? Caused by a direct blow to the skull, a concussion is a brain contusion that consequentially causes a total body shutdown. This can cause temporary or permanent damage, resulting in lengthy comas or even death. Isn't it amazing how a player can be big, fast, strong, smart, athletic, and everything else amazing … but then he or she can instantly be reduced to nothing by one ill-timed hit to the head? Once a player is concussed, it doesn't matter if he or she is multitalented.

The player can't use any of his or her skills while unconscious. I think we all know the importance of protecting our heads—but do we know the importance of protecting our heads spiritually?

God's team is issued helmets as well—the helmet of salvation. Obviously, the focus here is on salvation—but why a helmet? Well, whether it is the time leading up to accepting salvation through Christ or the life lived out after this acceptance, a person's head (our spiritual mind-set!) is the key to acceptance and understanding. We make the decision in our minds to accept or reject Christ, and then we use that same mind to decide throughout life whether or not we will remain faithful until the end.

How we use our minds to think and perceive determines the decisions we make in the game of life. This is why our playbook—Romans 12:2—says that we are transformed by the renewing of our minds, which helps us discern God's will for our lives. Jesus desires to completely change the way we think, because how we think inspires how we act.

Satan knows the importance of our minds as well. He also wants to influence how we think. That is why our heads are always the main focus of Satan's attacks. He is trying to give players on God's team a spiritual concussion, thus paralyzing our spiritual mind-sets for as long as he can. If Satan is successful in doing this, then he'll attempt to completely influence the way we think about life, people, God, Jesus, the Holy Spirit, money, sex, prestige—everything! He'll cleverly lead us into thinking that certain harmful things really won't hurt us, or he'll tell us that the sinful things we do are really not *that* bad.

This is why the helmet of salvation is so important; our minds will always be the main target. Jesus saved us, and that salvation is ours to either value or devalue. Satan's team will never stop attempting to influence us to lose appreciation for our salvation. If we leave our minds the slightest bit open to anything Satan has to say, he will take full advantage of it. Now, he can't steal our salvation, but he *can* steal other opportunities from us—such as our ability to make other disciples. We see this happen all the time in our world today when a Christian gives Satan too much room in his or her mind, allowing him to destroy his or her spiritual reputation. The world does not trust this Christian or his or her message, and Satan will have successfully rendered another Christian ineffective.

Even though Satan can't take your salvation, he will certainly try to influence you to give up on it; to give up on God, Jesus, and the Holy Spirit. He'll tempt you to lose faith; to quit the journey of growing in Christ; to stop following Jesus; to stop trusting the Holy Spirit's leading; and to quit the team. And he will use any means necessary to accomplish his evil agenda, as he prowls around like a roaring lion looking for unprotected heads. That's his game plan that he has stuck to since the beginning.

We know this because the Bible tells us that Satan also tried this with Jesus! Satan actually tried to get into the mind of our Lord and Savior Jesus Christ with the same schemes he uses to attack us today. Matthew tells us, "Again, the devil took him to a very high mountain and showed him all the kingdoms of the world and their splendor. 'All this I will give you,' he said, 'if you will bow down and worship me'" (Matthew 4:8–9).

This is just one of the multiple temptations that Satan threw at Jesus. If he'll try to make Jesus abandon the plan of God, then he will most certainly try to make you abandon it too! Of course, Jesus had His mind where it needed to be, and He demonstrated for us how to shut Satan down by using the Word of God. Now this same Jesus lives within us as our coach, and the same scriptures He blasted Satan with have become our playbook for the game of life! We can experience the same results Jesus did—making Satan flee. You do not have to grant him access to your mind!

Do not make the mistake of freely taking off your helmet of salvation by living too loosely and taking sin lightly! If we do that, we are only ripening ourselves for a spiritual concussion. We are not protecting our heads when we ignore the promptings of the Holy Spirit and become careless with movies, television, music, friends, language, and the Internet. We get loose and play with the gray areas of sin, and before we know it—boom!—Satan has taken control. It is then that we begin to think, act, and identify with Satan's team.

While we are spiritually concussed, Satan will try and do as much damage as he can, and when we finally come to, we find our lives have been turned upside down. Then Satan has us right where he wants us. If we lose hope, he's ready to pour on the power of guilt. Satan wants us to become too ashamed to talk to Jesus, prolonging repentance, while he happily continues to do damage.

The game of life is tough. Satan is tough. But Jesus is tougher still. That makes us tougher. If we keep our heads protected the way God's game plan commands, then we will stay sharp enough throughout our lives to finish the game strong.

Helmets in our sports do not prevent all head injuries, but they substantially limit the devastation (just try playing without one in a game that requires one!). Even with our helmets of salvation securely on our heads, we may still feel a few "headaches" from Satan's direct attacks on our minds, but he'll never knock us out. He'll never concuss us to the point of quitting God's team, as long as we keep that helmet of salvation on. For every trap Satan and his team tries to spring on us, Jesus has a solution—you can always count on pulling through:

> The temptations in your life are no different from what others experience. And God is faithful. He will not allow the temptation to be more than you can stand. When you are tempted, he will show you a way out so that you can endure. (1 Corinthians 10:13 NLT)

Did you catch that? God is faithful. He always provides a way out for the players on His team. Our coach cannot be outcoached by Satan. But when we are suffering from the symptoms of a spiritual concussion, the game plan of Jesus is more difficult to recognize. For this reason, remember to always spiritually protect your mind.

⏱ TIME-OUT

I'm going to veer a little off track with this time-out to hopefully drive the point home. What do you usually think about when you see people riding motorcycles at high speeds and have actually chosen to not wear a helmet? Don't they know what will happen if they crash? Do they care?

We think these people are crazy for what they are doing,

right? Living riskily, dangerously, and even recklessly. That is exactly the same thing we should think about Christians who toy around with what goes in and out of their minds on a daily basis. The way we think is nothing to play with.

🔳 DISCUSSION QUESTION

1. This discussion period will center around one central idea that will give you plenty to discuss: What kind of music do you listen to? What type of movies or television shows do you watch? What kind of books or magazines do you read? What kind of video games do you play? What are your social media habits? What kind of websites do you visit? What kind of social activities do you attend? Discuss these with others on your team. Satan tries to influence them all, so you need to decide: are the things I am consuming with my mind good or bad?

▶️ WATCH THE WRAP-UP VIDEO

To watch the wrap-up video, go to www.tcstallings.com, and on the "Playing on God's Team" page, click "Wrap-Up Vids." Then watch the video entitled Sessions #16–17: The Uniform, Part 2.

THE ARMOR OF GOD: THE SWORD

In football, when the quarterback handed me the ball during a game and I began to run, I would instantly become the focus of the entire defense. They were all on edge while I sprinted toward them, assessing how I might attack. Would I try to run around them with speed or run through them with power? They would follow my every move as they closed in on me. They had to stop me as fast as they possibly could. Why? It was because I was a threat, because I had the ball.

As long as I had the ball firmly in my hand, I could attack the defense and do damage. But what would happen if I fumbled and no longer had the ball? Would I be a threat any longer? No. Could I do damage? Of course not. Am I still the focal point of the entire defense? Not really. The moment I lost the ball, I became powerless, meaningless, and no threat to the defense whatsoever.

The same holds true on God's team. We have been given a weapon, which Paul calls the sword of the Spirit and which he further defines as the Word of God (see Ephesians 6:17). It is the Word of God that makes us a threat to Satan. By knowing the truth, power, provisions, and promises found in Scripture, we gain power against our enemy. By studying the ways of Jesus—His passions, His goals, His mannerisms, His choices, and His love for others—we gain power over the opposing team. When we choose to believe what Scripture says about our gifts, talents, abilities, and purposes, then we gain power against Satan!

It is by no coincidence that the analogy here is a sword, which is a weapon, because it's the way Team Jesus attacks. But as good as all of this sounds, why do we find so many people trying to be Christians without a commitment to reading God's Word? This is a big problem that only continues to grow because self-logic and personal opinions have replaced sound teaching these days. But our own ideas are no threat to Satan any more than I would be a threat to the defense as a running back without the ball. If we have no weapon, then we are not a threat—we can't do anything for Jesus without the power, guidance, and truth of God's Word.

Not only does the Bible provide a weapon against Satan, but it also helps us fight our worst enemy, which is ourselves. We have a heart that can be deceitful, a tongue that can speak evil, and a nature that is deeply rooted in sin. We need to understand this about ourselves or we will never truly see our need for Jesus in the first place. We'll keep telling ourselves that we are good people. We've all thought this at one time or another, which is why the Word of God is essential.

God's Word cuts through all the false layers of our lives, exposing the truth, and shows us who we really are. The writer of Hebrews reminds us of the exposing power of God's Word when he writes: "For the word of God is alive and powerful. It is sharper than the sharpest two-edged sword, cutting between soul and spirit, between joint and marrow. It exposes our innermost thoughts and desires" (Hebrews 4:12 NLT).

My message to you in this session is simple but serious.

Just as batters actually need bats to officially call themselves batters, so Christians need Bibles to call themselves Christians. No defense fears, respects, or takes seriously a so-called "batter" if they come to the plate without a bat—as if by gloved hands alone they have the potential of knocking one out of the park. And neither will Satan ever fear, respect, or take seriously the attack of a Bible*less* believer. Notice I did not say Bible*less Christian*. That is because there is no such thing. A *Christian* means "Christ follower"—and you can't follow Christ without a sword in your hand. All true Christians will have one and use it!

The Bible should be more than just a book people get as a baptism gift. It is a weapon with which we are to fight—it is designed to help us attack all areas of life. Paul reminded Timothy of this fact when he wrote:

> You have been taught the holy Scriptures from childhood, and they have given you the wisdom to receive the salvation that comes by trusting in Christ Jesus. All Scripture is inspired by God and is useful to teach us what is true and to make us realize what is wrong in our lives. It corrects us when we are wrong and teaches us to do what is right. God uses it to prepare and equip his people to do every good work. (2 Timothy 3:15–17)

If we are to be victorious in our Christian lives, then we need to take up the sword of the Spirit as part of our uniform, for it is the Word of God that has power to overcome the enemy.

⏱ TIME-OUT

By now we have reiterated a couple of key things about the Bible: It's the playbook for the game plan of life, and it's a multipurpose weapon. It has power ... but that is only if it's trusted and utilized. A commitment to trust and utilize God's Word has to be made in the heart of each and every person on God's team. Christians are invited to trust, read, obey, and depend upon all of Scripture. This is a nonnegotiable if we are to be followers of Jesus Christ.

🖼 DISCUSSION QUESTIONS

1. If someone asked you, "What does the Bible mean to you?" how would you answer?

2. How do you usually feel after reading Scripture? Motivated? Convicted? Confused? Inspired? How do you handle these feelings?

3. We all will keep studying and growing in Scripture, of course, but do you feel that you have a good enough grip on Scripture to effectively lead others to Christ? To help a struggling Christian? To consistently call on the truths in Scripture to fend off spiritual attacks?

4. Is the Bible your go-to method for guidance in every area of your life? How do you use it?

5. What has the truth of Scripture revealed about you to yourself? What changes have the truths of Scripture caused you to make in your own life? Have you personally had the opportunity to use the Bible to make a change in the life of someone else?

▶ WATCH THE WRAP-UP VIDEO

To watch the wrap-up video, go to www.tcstallings.com, and on the "Playing on God's Team" page, click "Wrap-Up Vids." Then watch the video entitled Session #18: The Sword.

PRAYER: IN-GAME COMMUNICATION

And pray in the Spirit on all occasions with all kinds of
prayers and requests. With this in mind, be alert and
always keep on praying for all of the Lord's people.
—Ephesians 6:18

We've already had one session on prayer, and it's so important that we are going to do another one. But this time we will focus on prayer as a weapon.

The armor of God includes prayer as part of the strategy with which we defeat the enemy; communication with Jesus is the power behind it! It is important that we understand this. Being able to constantly talk directly to Jesus in prayer is the most powerful privilege imaginable. We can ask Him to guide every move we make and take the lead in every area of our lives. How great is that! No guesswork is necessary; just pray and ask Him for wisdom. The Bible says that God freely gives wisdom to anyone who asks Him in faith (see James 1:5). Knowing that we can consult God about absolutely anything and are guaranteed wisdom concerning our questions should motivate us to pray in every circumstance in which we find ourselves.

Simply put, to not communicate with God is like ignoring the head coach during the game. It's just not going to work. Imagine a basketball game in which the score is tied with ten seconds left, and it is in the third overtime. The coach is using a time-out to draw up the perfect offensive play. At the end of the time-out, the players take the floor. Everyone is in position, including the defense. Then, just before the referee blows the whistle to resume play, the defense suddenly shifts. The offensive players get confused—they have never seen this shift before. It's a trap, and if the ball is thrown in, it's a steal for the defense. The head coach quickly notices this, has a plan B prepared, and screams out to the player inbounding the ball to call another time-out. But the player pridefully waves the coach off and says, "No, I got this." Man, I tell you what—he better have it!

In that scenario, maybe the player throws the ball into a trap, but maybe not. That's not the point. The point is that by ignoring the coach, the player leaves everything to chance. We can't do this in sports, and we definitely can't afford to leave our spiritual lives to chance either. Trying to live off luck, logic, and emotion—anything but prayer—will fail when trying to follow Jesus.

Instead, we should actually be motivated to pray all of the time, with guarantees in Scripture such as this to count on: "Do not be anxious about anything, but in every situation, by prayer and petition, with thanksgiving, present your requests to God. And the peace of God, which transcends all understanding, will guard your hearts and your minds in Christ Jesus" (Philippians 4:6–7).

On God's team, there are no true spiritual victories in life if communication from the coach is cut off. None. However, there is constant victory in the lives of those who value prayer and always put it first. Do not be like so many others who depend on talent, ambition, strength, courage, desire, endurance, strategy, or emotion to make decisions. These are all great traits, but only Jesus—the author of our lives—knows exactly how we should use them.

Never ignore Jesus.

Stay in communication all game long.

He plans; we pray. He coaches; we play.

⏱ TIME-OUT

I've tried to do my own thing a time or two in a football game. Although the coach had taught me how he wanted it done, I'd occasionally try something different. Maybe you've done this too in your own life. Sometimes it works out and we get credit for having "good instincts." That's fine when it comes to sports, but our instincts are useless in replacing the plans of Jesus. The best way to live life as a Christ follower on God's team is to leave all the play calling, adjustments, and strategizing up to Him (which keeps our plans from getting in the way).

▨▨ DISCUSSION QUESTIONS

1. Describe a particular situation in which you experienced Jesus leading you—all the way—from start to finish. How did it feel?

2. Can you think of a time when you went against the coach's play call? What happened? What about a time in which you spiritually went against what you knew was right? What happened in that case?

3. What do you think is more important: the team with the most talent or the team with the best strategy?

▸ WATCH THE WRAP-UP VIDEO

To watch the wrap-up video, go to www.tcstallings.com, and on the "Playing on God's Team" page, click "Wrap-Up Vids." Then watch the video entitled Session #19: Prayer: In-Game Communication.

THE WRAP UP: PREGAME SPEECH

I once saw a motivational video that grabbed my attention. To sum it up, it was about a player who asked a coach to help him become a champion. The coach agreed to personally help. So day after day the coach would use some of the most grueling and challenging methods while training him. But one day, the coach took things to another level.

At one training session, the coach took the player by the head and led him to a basin of water. After telling him to hold his breath, the coach dunked the player's head underneath the water for several seconds while the player held his breath. The coach pulled him up, waited briefly, and then put him under again for nearly a minute. The player became just a little uncomfortable, but held firm the entire time. The coach brought him up for air once again. One final time the coach put him under, but this time for well over a minute. The player began to feel uncomfortable. Fear set in, and he tried to come up for air. But the coach applied enough force to keep him fully submerged. The player went into a panic and began swinging his arms aggressively and grabbing the coach's arm desperately. Finally, just before he passed out, the coach let the player up for air. The coach then looked him in the eyes and said, "When you want to be a champion as bad as you just wanted to breathe, then you will be successful."

This video was more of a scripted motivational skit, and not an actual training scenario. But still—it's a pretty intense illustration, right? It makes the point for sure. But here's what really got my attention. This video received tons of "likes" and great comments. And I know why. As athletes and coaches, we love winning. We are in favor of situations that contribute to victory, no matter the challenge it presents.

People watching the video understood and supported its purpose—to show that anything less than our best is unacceptable. Poor effort is never tolerated in the world of sports. And neither is a lack of passion, discipline, strength, courage, endurance, goals, commitment, intelligence, character, or unity. You're expected to fail without them as an athlete. So my question is, what makes us think that a lack of these same qualities will be sufficient to play on God's team? This is the lie that has weakened us and misrepresented our coach.

Jesus wants our complete best and He deserves nothing less. But we have not committed to giving Him what He wants! What would happen if Christians wanted to obey Jesus more than we wanted to breathe? What would that even look like in the world? Do you think that would be overdoing it? Is God asking too much of us? I don't believe He is. He is simply calling on you to do for Him what you do every day in athletics. Go hard.

He knows you have the ability to go all out for Him. You are constantly asked to do it in sports, and you do it. Jesus asks the same—and He deserves it more. But are you going all out for Him?

As an athlete, you may have heard several pregame speeches over the years. It is the coach trying to put the seriousness of the game into perspective, and get you as ready as possible to play well. Consider this session as the same thing. I truly want you to play well for God's team. And as we get ready to wrap up, I want to encourage and challenge all of you to respond like a champion to this one final thought.

The grace you brag about, the grace that you are so thankful for and have so much appreciation for, the grace that changed your life, the grace that made you whole, the grace that paid your death penalty, the grace that made you holy in the sight of God, the grace that created an eternal home for you, and the grace of our Lord and Savior Jesus Christ should be the same grace that inspires you, drives you, motivates you, and energizes you to respond to Jesus with nothing but your best. And with all you have to give.

Like Paul said, we play hard for an earthly crown that will not last. But on God's team, we do it for a crown that lasts forever, for eternity. So let's play the hardest we've ever played before.

⏱ TIME-OUT

What kind of player would Jesus say you are? Regardless of your answer, after working through these twenty-one sessions you now know the kind of player God expects you to be on His team! With everything you've got, go do the work that He has prepared, ordained, and called you to do. As we all play on God's team each day, let the goal of hearing Him say, "Well done," be the driving force behind the way we live our lives! Always play hard and always play His way!

▶ WATCH THE WRAP-UP VIDEO

To watch the wrap-up video, go to www.tcstallings.com, and on the "Playing on God's Team" page, click "Wrap-Up Vids." Then watch the video entitled Session #20: The Pregame Speech.

SESSION 21

REFLECTION AND CELEBRATION: A CLOSING VIDEO

Team, I have a special closing message for you to watch, and then after viewing it, I would like for you to use this session to discuss what the last twenty weeks have meant to you. How have you grown? How do you feel now as opposed to when you first began? What spiritual victories have you experienced? What are you most excited about moving forward? This last session is all about reflection and celebration. It's also a time to encourage one another as you get ready to utilize what you've learned.

I could not be more proud to have been a part of your spiritual training sessions. I'll get even more joy out of watching you stand strong and victorious, each day, as champions in the game of life. God bless!

In Jesus' name we pray,
and on His team we play!
—T. C. Stallings

Watch the Official Closing Video

To watch the official closing video by T. C., go to www.tcstallings.com, and on the "Playing on God's Team" page, click "Wrap-Up Vids." Then watch the video entitled Session #21: The Official Closing Video.

RENEW YOUR COMMITMENT TO GOD'S TEAM

If you feel that you have not been giving Jesus your all, and you feel the need to recommit to doing so, then don't delay. That feeling is there for a reason. Respond now by asking Jesus to forgive you for taking the lead in your life, and simply ask Him to take it back. Tell Him whatever else is on your heart. Talk to Him just as if He were sitting in the room with you. Then be sure to ask Him for the strength to commit to staying behind Him from now on.

I encourage you to write down your recommitment to Jesus Christ. We athletes love to hang our goals where we can see them so I suggest you do the same with this recommitment, as the goal is to follow through with it. You can be sure that this goal of yours is definitely one that Jesus will help you achieve because it matches up with His plan for your life. Congrats on having the humility and courage to get real with yourself and God today!

Commit Your Life to God's Team

If you have never accepted Jesus Christ as your personal Lord and Savior and you feel a prompting to do so today, then this moment is for you. Right now, if you pray and ask Jesus to forgive you of all of your sins, believe in His death, burial, and resurrection, and humbly acknowledge Him as Lord and Savior, then you will indeed be saved. Take a moment, in your own way and with your own words, to do so right now.

If you just prayed and truly accepted Jesus as your Lord and Savior, then know that I am extremely excited for you. And I'm proud to call you a teammate in Christ!

ABOUT THE AUTHOR

T. C. Stallings is an actor, speaker, author, and former professional athlete in the Canadian, Arena, and European football leagues. He was a standout football player and active participant with Fellowship of Christian Athletes at the University of Louisville, and played high school football at his beloved Bedford High School in Bedford Heights, Ohio.

T. C. has experienced being a Christian athlete on all levels—from little league to the pros. His hopes are to use his experiences to help build true Christian athletes who can stand strong for Jesus on and off the field. He lives with his beautiful wife and his two wonderful children in Southern California. T. C. currently competes in USATF Master's Track and Field events as a sprinter. His favorite athlete of all time is the great Barry Sanders.